The Administrative Side of Coaching: A Handbook for Applying Business Concepts to Coaching Athletics

Date Due

The Administrative Side of Coaching: A Handbook for Applying Business Concepts to Coaching Athetics

Richard Leonard

Fitness Information Technology
A Division of the International Center for Performance Excellence
262 Coliseum, WVU-PE
PO Box 6116
Morgantown, WV 26506-6116

Library of Congress Card Catalog Number: 2001012345
ISBN: 1885693540

Production Editor: Geoffrey C. Fuller
Cover design: 40 West Studios
Typesetter: Jamie Pein
Printed by Data Reproductions
Printed in the United States of America

10 9 8 7 6 5 4 3 2 1

Fitness Information Technology
A Division of the International Center for Performance Excellence
262 Coliseum, WVU-PE
PO Box 6116
Morgantown, WV 26506-6116 USA
800.477.4348 (toll free)
304.293.6888 (phone)
304.293.6658 (fax)
Email: fit@fitinfotech.com
Website: www.fitinfotech.com

Preface ....

In developing this book, I was confronted with two explicit questions. First and foremost, will this composition be received in the spirit that it was written? Secondly, will coaches and athletic administrators of today be interested in the sum and substance of it? Let's address the second question first: Will coaches and administrators be interested in the subject matter?

Anyone who has spent time in coaching and program administration (no matter what the sport or level of competition) realizes that while a competent knowledge of his or her sport is imperative for achievement and success, coaching goes far beyond diagramming Xs and Os, teaching innovative playing techniques, or designing unique variations of a practice drill. Whether one acknowledges it or not, all coaches perform the same obligatory duties as managers in the business world. Like business managers, coaches and athletic program administrators are individuals of responsibility who act as facilitators, decision makers, and resource allocators with both formal and informal authority. It is important to break down this last statement into its simplest terms so the connection between business management and athletic coaching/administration can be clearly seen.

As facilitators, business managers are responsible for the orderly operation of their respective division, facility, or company. Coaches and athletic program administrators are no different. They must ensure their program's consistent functioning in everything from practice to competition, player to player (or coach) relations, facility scheduling, fundraising, and countless other administrative elements. From the perspective of decision making, business managers are directly accountable for both primary and secondary decisions that not only influence the prevailing situation but the future direction of the organization. Coaches and athletic program administrators also make consequential decisions on a daily basis that determine a program's current and future success. Additionally, business managers and coach-administrators are also responsible for all types of resource allocations. Resources such as time, money, and manpower are important for both to distribute equitably and appropriately for the business or athletic program to function effectively. Finally, business managers and coach-administrators are similar in regard to formal and informal authority. Whether one is a corporate manager or a coach or athletic administrator, there is certain, inherent, formal jurisdictional power in the organizational position and title. How one handles the explicit authority is determined by personal style and specific situation, but it is legitimized through job responsibilities and duties. On the other side of the coin is informal authority, which both managers and coaches promote through their distinct personalities. Informal power is what motivates employees (or in our case, athletes and staff) to achieve beyond required expectations. Successful managers and coaches/program administrators have the intangible talent to inspire and focus employees and athletes.

Another significant parallel that exists between the business world and our profession of coaching athletics relates to the intense search for a competitive edge. In every business environment, corporate managers understand the urgency associated with operational efficiency. They understand how a skillful deployment of administrative fundamentals can and will provide a practical advantage over the competition. The same philosophy applies to coaching.

Athletic programs, whatever the level or sports, are experiencing an exponentially increasing volume and concentration of competition. Coaches no longer have the luxury of managerial complacency. In simple terms, to endure, athletic programs must be as administratively competent as possible. The application of business techniques discussed in this book could be the difference between survival and growth and deterioration and failure.

In response to my initial concern of whether this book will be received in the spirit that it was written, I would sincerely like to see it used as a generator of good ideas for improving a coach's/athletic administrator's work and personal life. Ideas produce movement. Good ideas create movement, which, in turn, creates progress. From that premise, the book could be utilized as a reference or as a cover-to-cover foundation for program and team administration. No matter how one utilizes this text, if it produces new good thinking, then it is a success.

Contents ....

Detailed Contents ....

Chapter 9: Athletic Program Promotion and Marketing Communication 121

Chapter 10: Public Relations in Sports Programs 133

Chapter 13: Strategic Management and Coaching 169

Chapter 14: Business Ethics and Coaching 181

Section V: Appendix 187

Section VI: Suggested Readings 193

About the Author 201

Figure List ....

Chapter 8

Chapter 9

Chapter 10

Chapter 11

Chapter 12

Chapter 13

Chapter 14

Section I ....
Management Concepts for Coaches

Section I Management Concepts for Coaches

As discussed in the introduction, coaches and program administrators should have a pragmatic knowledge of business principles not only to run day-to-day team and program operations but to supply long-term vision and direction to all program members. By far the most important of all business disciplines for a coach or program administrator is the interrelated foundations of management.

In his 1993 graduate text Management, Arthur Bedeian breaks down management into five progressive, interconnected functions: Planning, Organization, Human Resource Management, Leadership, and Control:

a. Planning is the process of establishing goals and selecting a course of action to accomplish these goals.

b. Organization is the process of dividing work among individuals and groups and coordinating their activities to accomplish goals.

c. Human Resource Management is the process of ensuring that employees are selected, developed, and rewarded for accomplishing goals.

d. Leadership is the process of inducing individuals or groups to assist in accomplishing goals.

e. Control is the process of ensuring the accomplishment of goals.

This section comprehensively examines these five functions of management as they relate to coaching and program administration.

Chapter 1 ....

Planning

Objectives

- To introduce the concept of planning as it relates to athletics.
- To provide a sectional structure for program planning.
- To elaborate on and stress the importance of the following components of a program plan:
    - Mission statements
    - Program chronicled description
    - Program structure
    - Goal setting
    - Rules and operating actions
    - Marketing formation
    - Financial reporting
    - Supplementary information
- To furnish benefits and applications of program planning.

Introduction

While planning is conceivably the most significant ingredient in the management process, it is undoubtedly the one element that triggers the most frustration and anxiety. One often hears the expression "the future is uncertain." As human beings, we try to avoid uncertainty while attempting to prolong the established and known. However, the essential makeup of business forces managers to proactively recognize and take hold of the future. Planning is that practical managerial function that deals with strategies to minimize the impact of the unknown. Planning also provides the organization with a tangible shared vision that all stakeholders can reference and follow. This collective focus reduces the unproductive use of time, materials, manpower, and finances.

The planning function ranks among the most significant in thriving corporate settings. For our task as coaches and administrators, it can be simplified into these basic factors:

- Objectives and goals to be sought.
- Policies to be followed.
- Organizational structure.
- Resources to be utilized.
- Environmental/external factors to be handled (Jucius, Dietzer, and Bernard, 1973).

These five components are found in virtually every type of business planning process. The configuration and interpretation of each of these items, as well as their utilization, change from organization to organization.

Athletic Program Planning

The most lucid and understandable way to structure the five factors of planning is through an instrument called a business operational plan or, for our purposes, an athletic program plan. Figure 1 is an illustration of how one could arrange an athletic program plan.

Figure 1: Athletic Program Plan Sectional Breakdown

Section 1: Mission Statement
Section 2: Program History
Section 3: Executive Summary/Organizational Chart
Section 4: Long-Term Program Goals (3-5 years)
Section 5: Short-Term Program Goals (1-2 year actions)
Section 6: Policies and Procedures
Section 7: Marketing and Promotional Plan
Section 8: Financial Projections/Fundraising Programs
Section 9: Appendix

Before a clarification is given to these components of the athletic program plan, it is imperative that one recognize that program plans are group endeavors and they must have everyone's total pledge and commitment. The document can not be a single person's perspective, but the vision of everyon involved with the operation and administration of the program. Whether one is running a junior, high school, college, or professional program, the participatory involvement of coaches, parents, administrators, and athletes is vital for planning and goal fulfillment.

The following sections (based on figure 1) will help a coach or program administrator assemble an athletic program plan.

SECTION 1: Mission Statement

A mission statement is defined as "a broad, unique aim that sets the organization apart from others of its type" (Stoner, 1978). In other words, a mission statement is an all-encompassing declaration that defines the overall purpose, philosophy, and vision of the organization and program. "It provides a foundation on which to build a future. . . it unifies the people in the organization. . . and provides the members [of the program] with a sense of direction" (Abrahams, 1995). All objectives, policies, procedures, and actions emanate from the mission statement.

There are countless books and related literature on business planning and the development of a mission statement. Each has its own style and design criteria for a mission statement. The format and wording used is a matter of personal preference and style. However, in writing the program's mission statement, answer the following broad but indispensable questions:

- What is our program about?
- What is our principal purpose?
- What is our philosophy in running our program?
- What is our operational environment?
- What is the future of our operations?

A mission statement can be as succinct and brief as a few sentences or as lengthy as a multipaged elaboration. A short, straightforward mission statement could be advantageous if the program plan is to be utilized for external funding and support. A multipage embellishment could be used to motivate internal staff and players by providing a comprehensive operational rationale and a philosophical course of action.

Administrative Tip

Do not hesitate to study other athletic program or business mission statements to come up with ideas and inspiration. Benchmarking mission statement format and content is a very viable method to formulate the program's own individualized mission. Annual reports, which contain business mission statements, are readily available at major public and university libraries.

SECTION 2: Program History

Developing a program history might seem unproductive to some coaches and administrators. In actuality, this section furnishes internal and external stakeholders, who are fundamentally defined as people who have any type of existing or future interest in the program (the internal are players and staff and the external are administrators and future sponsors), with a point of reference and a progressive framework which they can follow. There are many ways to arrange this section. It can be in narrative form, an outline, or even in a timeline style. More importantly, it should be in ascending chronological order from beginning to the present. The justification for compiling events this way is that a program plan is futuristic in nature. The plan should reflect where the program was, where it is, and where it will be.

SECTION 3: Key Players/Executive Summary/ Organizational Chart

The program plan segment titled Key Players/Executive Summary/ Organizational Chart has three independent but closely interconnected elements. The subsection of key players is a conventional job description behind each staff position in the organization (program director, head coach, newsletter publisher, public relations director, etc.). The second subsection, the executive summary, is an amplification of each specific person in these positions. This can be done through a resumé/vitae format or a brief historical narrative on each individual. The final subsection is a standard organizational chart. The diagram should display the hierarchical structure of the organization/program, who is accountable to whom, and who is answerable for each division below (chain of command). When combined together, these three elements provide everyone with clearly defined roles, positions, and program structure.

SECTIONS 4 and 5: Long- and Short-Term Goals

The next section of the program plan deals with substantial, tangible goals and objectives. Long-term goals are the program's aspirations while short-term goals are the sequence of specific actions to achieve those aspirations.

The program's goals and objectives reflect the primary program intentions and they determine both the itinerary and timetable for getting there. In other words, goals and objectives focus the company/program on the important work at hand and provide the mechanism for measuring progress (Tiffany and Peterson, 1997).

In essence, these two sections are the substance and heart of the program plan. Obviously, long-term goals (three- to five-year projections) will be broader in outlook. Short-term goals will be decisive actions that will be utilized to reach long-term objectives.

The actual makeup of each unique goal is up to the coaches or administrators, stakeholders, and the sport's nature. However, there are some integral parameters and rules that should be placed on establishing goals. They are as follows:

1. All goals should ultimately derive from the mission statement.
2. When formulating goals, long-term objectives should be defined first. Subsequently, short-term actions should be formulated regarding how to accomplish each long-term goal.
3. It is critical to base all goals in reality. It is necessary to ask the following questions:
   - Do we currently have the resources and funds to achieve our projected goals?
   - Do we have the potential to acquire the essential resources and funds to accomplish goals?
   - Do we have the staff or the likelihood of acquiring the staff to attain goals?

Administrative Tip

It is frequently asked, "How many long-term goals should our program develop and implement?" Because of the generalized nature of long-term goals as well as the limited resources of most sports programs, no more than 4 or 5 long-term goals should be attempted. How many short-term actions should be devised for each long-term goal? However many it takes to accomplish that long-term goal. Simply put, it may take a few short-term and immediate actions to reach a long-term goal or it could take dozens. It all depends on the long-term goal.

- Is the timeframe for the execution of the goals practical?
- Will there be any internal or external confrontations or resistance to the goals?

4. Goals should be easily comprehensible by everyone in the organization. They should be straightforward, concise, and in common language.

5. Each goal should be distinctive and salient. In other words, are the goals repetitive or are they unique in origin?

6. Each goal should have the absolute endorsement and focus of everyone in the organization. In the athletic program setting, the players/athletes, coaches, and administrators should be involved in the goal-setting process. Without everyone's input, key stakeholders might not take an active interest in operations, which, in turn, may leave goals unattained.

SECTION 6: Policies and Procedures

In his 1984 guidebook, *Business Policies and Procedure Handbook*, Steve Butler Page highlights the acute importance of developing program policies and procedures by stating that

> policies and procedures play a significant role in the company's environment in which employees/personnel make decisions. . . they provide decision makers with limits, alternatives, and general guidelines. . . they should be in writing to reduce the range of individual decisions. . . managers then will begin to make decisions that will be consistent from one function area to the next. The manager need only give special attention to unusual problems, not covered specifically by a policy or procedure.

While policies and procedures are ordinarily listed together in a program plan, they are two autonomous elements that facilitate an organization's effectiveness. *Policies* are defined as "broad guidelines to decisions and actions required in attaining organizational objectives. *Procedures* refers to a series of sequentially related steps that are followed to accomplish a given purpose" (Trewatha, 1979). In simplest terms, policies are more in line with program rules that guide behavior (people oriented) while procedures are narrow-scope steps/methods that explain how to perform program functions (task oriented).

As coaches, the most consequential aspect for the development and the use of policies would be dealing with players and staff members. The different areas in policy formulation and implementation concerning athletes would encompass all types of behavioral expectations. Some of these behavioral expectations are found in Figure 2.

Administrative Tip

Policy and procedure manuals are only beneficial if they are acknowledged, established, and applied. The commitment displayed by the coach or program administrator to policy and procedure manuals will determine the efficiency of the policies and procedures. Either through formal meetings or informal exchanges, constantly re-emphasize the program's commitment to its policies and procedures.

Figure 2: Athlete and Staff Behavioral Expectations

Players
Academics
Practice Policies
Tardiness/Absenteeism
Alcohol/Drugs
On Court/Field Disposition
Off Court/Field representation
Media Relations

Coaches/Staff
Player Relations
On and Off Court/Field Representation
Recruiting
Administrative Responsibilities

The concentration and range of policy items within a program plan are determined by the team's philosophies, position, operational environment, history, and traditions. Some areas maybe more accentuated than others. For example, an athletic program may be a university/college team or school where athletes have a documented history of alcohol abuse. In this case, the policies section of the program plan may elucidate specific policies on alcohol and drug abuse as well as detail a definitive warning/disciplinary system (verbal warnings, written warnings, suspension, expulsion) for violations. In such an environment, each program member should have an absolute understanding of the ramifications of alcohol and drug use. The program's alcohol and drug policies should be in lucid, plain language to avoid any misinterpretations.

Procedures are step-by-step actions taken to perform specific tasks. As coaches, we would like to see our programs establish straightforward procedures in areas of travel, purchasing, budgeting, cash handling, registration, and other administrative functions. The biggest dividend in determining procedures for administrative functions is uniformity. Uniformity saves time, coordinates activities, and minimizes frustration and stress that arise from disorganization.

SECTION 7: Marketing/Promotions

While Chapters 8, 9, and 10 will be devoted to marketing concepts and planning, it is meaningful to discuss them as a component of the program plan. The business discipline of marketing is broken down into four factors known as the 4Ps of marketing (or the marketing mix). The 4Ps:

Product

Price

Place

Promotion

The first of the 4Ps, product, is the one component we as coaches spend the greatest effort in developing. All other marketing activities stem from it. Our product is a quality athletic program and team. People (especially Americans) can occasionally be deceived into purchasing certain products that are of low caliber and value. The one product that this country seems to consume voraciously is entertainment. Athletics is entertainment. In the most elementary terms, if a team is not good, the public will stay away no matter what marketing strategies are employed. Does this mean that a program/team needs to be undefeated before people will pay notice or support it? No. It simply means that we need to be competitive and stimulating in various other ways to attract consumers and supporters.

The second of the 4Ps, price, derives from the same logic. The more in demand our product, the more flexibility in the price the consumer will pay for the product. Simply put, the more competitive the team, the more predisposed the consumer will be to pay a higher price to watch and support it.

The third of the 4Ps, place, is commonly determined by other external factors in athletics such as in what league, conference, or geographic region one's program is located. Place (or product distribution) proceeds from the logical reality that the more conspicuous and in-demand our program is, the more places we can sell it.

The final member of the 4Ps, promotion, is the one facet that coaches and administrators can, if properly directed, have the most affect on and is the one area of the marketing mix that needs to be expressly spelled out in our program plans. If one has a competent, quality product at an acceptable price and locale, then it is up to our own resourcefulness, creativity, and effort to promote it. Is funding consequential in promotion? It is significant but not imperative. Any advertising executive will communicate that the ultimate aspiration of any promotional campaign is to secure and enlarge positive word-of-mouth about the product. Can a program achieve this without major funding? Yes. Would it be easier to implement promotion with relevant funding? Undoubtedly. Yet, coaches cannot let funding be the stumbling block of promotion.

It should be restated that marketing will be presented in more detail later in the text. However, from a program plan perspective, one needs to distinguish what resources are going to be available for promotion and then formulate a strategy to augment every dollar allotted. For athletic programs with minimal dollars, concepts such as utilizing athletes (and families),

Administrative Tip

Never blindly leap into a marketing and promotions campaign. Too much is riding on the success or failure of marketing. It is the fastest way to squander a program's limited and most precious resource: money. Learn as much as possible about marketing theories. Enlist people with backgrounds in marketing to lend a hand to the program. Gain knowledge from the marketing achievements and disappointments of others. The time will be well spent.

developing distinct logos, composing and distributing fliers, and verbally publicizing the program and/or special events are pivotal. Additionally, one can persuade student groups, participate and attend charitable functions, make publicity speeches, utilize alumni groups and former players, build a rapport with local media, and develop a news release system. These are all cost effective techniques for program promotion. Once again, coaches and program personnel must be enterprising and imaginative.

After the foundations of the marketing mix have been developed, the marketing component of a program plan needs to be assembled. A coach or program administrator has two choices. The marketing section of an athletic program can

1. Embody and incorporate the entire comprehensive marketing plan of a program. These detailed documents break down the marketing mix:
   - Target marketing and demographics
   - Evaluation of competition
   - Customer profiles
   - Detailed elaboration of the marketing mix
2. Summarize the marketing plan. This strategy keeps marketing and its planning as an independent, particular document while providing a broad overview in the program plan.

SECTION 8: Financial Projections/Financial Statements

Financial projecting is budgeting. There are two direct ways of budgeting:

Method 1 - Assess and evaluate all of the program's expected expenditures, total the amount, and that result is the targeted income (break-even) amount.

Method 2 - Estimate the realizable income (or total money available) then attempt to adapt expenditures within that amount.

The budgeting concept is that simple. The quandary comes from how to arrive at one's conclusions and how precise one can be at predicting the future. A lucky few just know how to "guesstimate" and their approximations are, in general, accurate. The majority of us need to budget through concrete calculations.

While the budgeting concepts are covered in Chapters 6, 7, Appendix 7A, and Appendix 7B, there are some customary rules for deriving calculations and budget.

1. Base beginning projections in recorded facts. Usually the amount spent or received in previous years is a good basis.
2. Always forecast high on projected expenditures and low on projected income/revenue.
3. Get solid dollar amounts whenever possible. This might mean additional phone calls and leg work, but the effort will provide substantially more dependable projections. Furthermore, whenever conceivably possible, get all quotes in writing.
4. Always anticipate miscellaneous expenses. The amount of miscellaneous/float dollars should be projected at 5-10% of the total amounts.

5. Contemplate all budget line items before computing dollar amounts. Attempt to incorporate every realistic expense and income source.
6. Triple-check all calculations.
7. Keep organized files for back-up and confirmation of budget amounts.

The program plan should not only include the budget and projections, but also a short narrative explanation on each item and how those estimates were derived. While financial projections are future oriented, financial statements are historic records of what actually was received and expensed. The importance of including this type of information is in the validation of the current budget projections. Additionally, the quantitative comparison of what happened during the last fiscal period and what is predicted to happen this fiscal period provides the coach/program administrator an opportunity to explain variances.

The extent to which a coach budgets depends greatly on the type and size of the program as well on as the level of expertise a coach has in budgeting and financial statement accounting. The explanation of all of the different possible financial statements and quantitative forecasting techniques moves beyond the parameters of this manuscript. However, a fundamental working knowledge of budgeting (discussed later in this book) is critical for all coaches and program administrators.

SECTION 9: Appendix

The appendix section of a program plan can be just as important in providing salient information to stakeholders as the other sections. Information such as fundraising programs, travel itineraries, conditioning/training programs and schedules, booster programs and events, and volunteer activities are just a few of the elements that could be included in this section of the program plan. Once again, the extent of information provided in the appendix depends on numerous variables that are sport and program specific.

Administrative Tip

The appendix segment of a program plan is not a "junk drawer" section. Keep only salient information in it and maintain its organization.

Summary

There are distinct benefits and applications associated with developing a program plan. The predominant are
1. To furnish stakeholders with a concrete, tangible focus for the future.
2. To project professionalism to external groups and individuals.
3. To provide a valuable and useful tool for acquiring financial backing for the program.
4. To give staff members a sense of continuity.
5. To recruit new staff members or to recruit new athletes.
6. To provide the organization with a reality foundation. In other words, it simply distinguishes what can or cannot be accomplished.

The program plan is not a stagnate document. It should be considered an alterable and flexible plan that needs constant progressive updates and amendments. While most revisions will be minor modifications, they are indispensable in maintaining the ongoing benefits. The ability to adapt and change the program plan to the changing environment in athletics could mean the difference between a program's success or collapse.

APPENDIX A: Program Plan Outline

The following is a detailed sectional outline of a business plan that can be adopted in athletic programs. Note: There is no single standard format for a business plan. General sections are consistent but not order or format.

Business Plan Outline

I.   Title Page (appropriate creativity is a plus)
- Program name
- Logo
- Program business plan
- Completion/distribution date

II.   Table of Contents

III.   Company/Program Conceptual Description
- 1-Page Synopsis of
    - Nature of the program
    - Primary philosophy
    - Historical development
    - Location, competitive level, etc.

IV.   Mission Statement (vision, philosophy, major goal)
- An all-encompassing statement of philosophy, future vision, and major operational goal

V.   Long-Term Goals (3-5 years)
- 5 to 7 total long-term goals of the athletic program
- Broad but quantitative if possible

VI.   Short-Term Goals (1-2 years)
-   Take each long-term goal and have specific actions (this year or next to reach long-term objective
- Precise and measurable
- No set number—as many as needed to fulfill each long-term objective

VII.   Executive Summary
- Key players
- Job descriptions
- Hierarchical chart

VIII.   SWOT Analysis (optional) [To be discussed in Chapter 13]

IX.   Human Resource Plan
- All aspects of human resource to include
    Hiring procedures
    Staffing requirements
    Disciplinary/separation
    Compensation/benefits
- Policy and procedure manual

X.   Marketing Plan [To be discussed in Appendix 8A]

XI.   Financial Projections and Financial Statements

XII.   Appendix
- Supplementary information and materials
- Support data

Chapter 2 ....

Organization

Objectives

- To describe the foundations of personal and program organization.
- To analyze personal organization through time management methodologies.
- To examine office organization through filing, office flow, and computerization.
- To develop program organization by means of structure and power considerations.
- To investigate the organization of internal stakeholders through hierarchical systems, job designs, and job descriptions.
- To evaluate external stakeholders and to organize, manage, and control them.

Introduction

Chapter 1 in this book reviewed the first of the five managerial tasks: planning. This chapter accentuates the managerial function of organization. The section probes personal organizational techniques as well as program organization and design structure. In the truest application of the organizational function in the management process, the concept of organization is formally associated with the blueprint configuration of the business (in our case, athletic program). However, for our purposes, the meaning of the term organization encompasses personal as well as athletic program organization. The relevant rationale is that one's personality and individual performance can have a direct correlation to the prosperity of a program. Simply put, if the coach or program administrator is an organized and structured individual, the program will be organized and structured. Unfortunately, in this scenario, the inverse is also true.

Personal Organization

Personal organization is an exceptionally subjective topic. Tactics that can be useful for enhancing one person's performance might not work well for another. To discover if one is personally organized, ask some elementary, point-blank questions:

1. Is work getting done in a timely manner?
2. Is there spare time during the day to sit back and examine overall program direction and goals or is one constantly inundated with daily assignments that seem endless?
3. Can pertinent materials and data be retrieved instantaneously?
4. Is one always rushing to get to critical engagements and meetings?
5. Is it possible to manipulate and control the length and content of meetings? Of phone calls?
6. When leaving the program at night, does one feel prepared for the next day?

If not satisfied with the answers to the above questions, a coach or program administrator can explore the potential of improving personal organization in two important areas: time management and office organization.

Time Management

The most precious commodity we all have is time. In some cases, the sheer magnitude of work will dictate the availability of coaching and professional time. In most other instances, a coach can have a direct influence on time control and planning. This is where the much elaborated concept of time management comes into play. Time management

> is the proactive technique of taking control of daily demands and interruptions. . . offensively and actively shaping the day. The key is to establish selective control: refocus and harness the time one can control and institute defensive measures to minimize the impact of demands that can not be controlled (Winston, 1985).

The repercussions of time management and the effective utilization of time have been a source of managerial focus and research for decades. As the program administrator, consolidate and emphasize time planning in all operational functions.

Time management consists of three fundamental steps:

1. Determine how time is being used.
2. Analyze and evaluate current time usage.
3. Develop an improvement plan" (Carlisle, 1987).

For trivial tasks, these three steps can literally take a matter of seconds to contemplate and achieve. For larger roles and responsibilities, one will need to outline a course of action.

The first two steps in the time management process are strictly seen from a situational and contemplative personal standpoint. In other words, only an individual can determine how his or her time is being applied and if the application is adequate. If it is perceived that the time usage is lacking, then the development of an improvement strategy would be an advantage.

In his 1986 self-help book, *The Management Handbook*, Arthur Young presents 18 tips for time management and time improvement planning.

- Define the essentials of the job. Ensure that a majority of the time is spent on them.
- Ration all program players and staff time. Arrange schedules so that top-priority items are dealt with when people are at their best.
- Gradually allow less time for tasks as experience increases until optimum performance is reached.
- Show disapproval of wasting time.
- Always question the importance of specific tasks. They may be irrelevant and capable of being postponed.
- Before committing to a task, check to see if it can be delegated.
- Conduct brief meetings; set time limits for objectives.
- Try to protect productive time from intrusions.
- Make it known that one's time is precious so that others compete and negotiate for it.
- Always thank others for being brief and to the point.
- Spend time understanding the organization.
- Minimize the time players and staff spend on unpopular tasks.
- Spend time on understanding one's profession.
- Encourage enthusiasm; it makes people work faster.
- Create surges of activities toward goals.
- Set deadlines for oneself as well as players and staff, but always remember that speed is not the only consideration, particularly if quality suffers.
- Constantly question if an activity is the best use of time.

There are auxiliary tools that can be utilized to systematize time and activities:

1. A List of Things to Do: This list can be ordered by function, priority, or duration of assignments and tasks. The simplest, most valuable method is the three-point priority system. On a daily basis, write a master list of things to do. Even if the list is practically identical to the day prior, rewriting it on a daily basis reaffirms responsibilities and appointments. While writing the list, leave the left margin open. After the list is completed, go through each line item and numerically order them on importance and gravity. An item or task that has critical consequences should be numbered with a 1. A 2 article is a midrange element that has significance but is not an imperative priority. Obviously, a 3 duty is a low concern that does not necessitate immediate attention. The other purpose for rewriting the list on a continual basis is to re-rank objectives and duties. For example, a 3-priority task could suddenly become a 1-priority overnight or vice versa. Another modification could be to date each item or responsibility on its projected or required completion date. As soon as a task is completed,

Administrative Tip

Ask diligent, industrious people outside the program how they manage their time. Pose specific questions that relate to the programs operations and how they would handle the time constraints. Inquire what one of their typical days is like. From these explorations, form time management improvement techniques.

There are two central points to skillful time management. The first is to find out what works properly for one's style, and the second is to find out what works acceptably for the program's position of coach or program administrator. Correlate and modify those two outlooks to form a distinct and comfortable routine. Remember that one distinct approach to time management might be suitable for one particular setting (or individual) but not for another. Time management, as most management techniques, is situational.

mark it off. It is often a good idea to maintain a file of preceding lists to substantiate task completion and dates.

2. Daily Schedules/Daily Planner: The daily planner can be used to coordinate the list of things to do (master list). The integration of the list of things to do with a daily calendar can give one the flexibility to schedule future tasks on the date when work is planned to start" (Mayer, 1995). Breaking this concept down, arrange the day alongside the list of things to do. It does not have to be an intricate, minute by minute time table; rather a generalized time schedule. When planning out the day, one should always attempt to leave an open-door period during which the program's staff and athletes have an opportunity to discuss their concerns and problems.

3. Screen Calls: Plan in the daily agenda time to return calls. If possible, screen calls for their importance. An urgent message warrants immediate attention, while a low priority messages should be returned afterward.

4. Rechannel Unscheduled Visitors to Open Time Slots: This is more precarious than screening calls simply because of the face-to-face predicament. Initially, weigh out the cost and benefit of an unscheduled "drop in." If it is perceived that an unscheduled visitor could have a substantial benefit, the conversation mandates direct, uninterrupted attention. It should be noted that if you evaluate the benefits of a conversation and feel that it is necessary, you should give that individual your undivided attention. If not, the conversation will be costly in respect to time as well as detrimental to the future relationship with that individual.

5. Alternate Work Site: Try to maintain a discrete, alternate work area if possible. As devious as this seems, attempt to find an inconspicuous and obscure corner to get away from "no win" time periods. A "no win" time period is one where priorities are outstanding and interruptions are many. Have an office or staff confidant involved at all times in case of any contingent emergencies.

Office Organization

Once again, how one arranges one's office or work area is purely a subjective preference. Does a clean office necessarily mean an organized, proficient office? Not necessarily. We have all known people whose work areas could be pronounced disaster zones, but when asked, they could find an obscure object or document processed six months earlier. On the other hand, there are people whose offices and desks are so tidy that they could land a plane on them, but they never seem to be able to locate anything that they are looking for. Whatever works is the primary consideration.

The following are principal factors and components of office organization:

1. Filing systems
2. Pitch system

3. Office flow
4. Computers

Filing Systems

Because of the escalating popularity of personal computers, filing now has evolved into a question of which floppy disk or hard drive contains which file of information. However, even with the most reliable computer systems, it is crucial that a "hard copy" filing system (tangible backup copy, typically a printout or other paper document of pertinent data) be maintained. These materials must be cataloged in such a way that they can be located instantaneously with little or no effort by all staff members associated with the program. The cardinal rule of filing is "the simpler the better." Expenditures associated with filing systems can be minimal. If ordered correctly, a five-drawer cabinet with basic hanging file folders can be more than enough.

To install a filing system, one needs to identify paramount program categories first and work toward smaller details within each classification. Hopefully, the program will not have more than five or six dominant classifications. For example, for most athletic programs, some of the major categories could be *player files*, *travel files*, *home event files*, *recruiting files*, and *staff and general administration files*.

Player files can be subsectioned into groups (age, position, school status) or could be filed aggregately. Whether subsectioned or not, these files should be in alphabetical order and as comprehensive as possible. Attempt to standardize basic information for each file and player. For example, a coach or program administrator might consider it essential that each athlete's file incorporate class schedules, medical information, emergency contacts, conditioning plans, etc. After the standardized data has been uniformly filed, supplement each file with other subsequent individualized information.

Travel files must be maintained with diligence. These files should be categorized by dates in ascending order. Pertinent information such as confirmation documentation, contracts, directions, itineraries, and emergency phone numbers could be included.

Home event files are not as essential to most athletic programs as player and travel files but are still meaningful to sustain. Home files, like travel files, should be in ascending order of event dates. They could incorporate schedules, event protocols, competition contracts, and miscellaneous data on incoming teams.

The materials contained in recruit files are often ordered by the governing body of the organization in which the program competes (State High School Association, NCAA, National Leagues, NJCAA, professional organizations, NAIA, etc.). These files could be arranged by recruit class and contain information on each prospect's individual strengths and significance.

Staff and general administration files can comprise an extensive variety of data. Program components such as budgeting and financial information,

Administrative Tip

The importance of precision and orderliness in a filing system can never be overestimated. A disorderly and haphazard filing system can actually be worse than having no filing system at all. Reiterate to every staff member whohas access to the program's filing system that not only is security a primary ingredient of filing but so is neatness.

Administrative Tip

Accessibility of archived files should be in reverse chronological order, with the most recent years the easiest to retrieve. Furthermore, just because files are archived does not mean that their organization and accuracy is not essential. Their preservation is just as important as that of active files.

promotional activities, mailing lists and booster/alumni contacts, and updated departmental memos can be included in this filing category. It is also recommended that these files be sorted alphabetically.

Once the system has been refined, it is imperative that all files are intermittently cleaned out. Files have a tendency to get cluttered with obsolete materials. Appropriate maintenance means going through each one and thinning out nonpertinent information. Additionally, at the end of the fiscal or competitive year, pull out yearly files and archive and store them for future reference. Even though it is up to one's personal preference, it is advisable to retain archived files for at least three years.

To conclude this section, Odett Pollar, in her 1992 guidebook: *Organizing Your Work Space*, gives 5 common mistakes with filing:

1. Not remembering how items are categorized.
2. Creating a good system but not keeping up with it.
3. Creating a file for every type of document (lots of files with only one document in them).
4. Files with long, convoluted titles.
5. Filing indefinitely with no provision for purging files.

Each of these oversights and mistakes in filing can be overcome with some straightforward practices:

1. To keep track of the categories of items filed and to be filed, post a single sheet of paper alongside the file cabinet with the categories and their breakdown. The filing breakdown could be in a simplified outline form. In addition to being a reference, the sorting document could act as a method of designating file names appropriately.
2. To keep up the filing system and adequately purge files, schedule times to routinely review the filing system. The times could be standardized from week to week or could be by a once-a-month, open-time schedule. It is advisable not to let files go unattended for over one month.

Pitch Method

Administrative Tip

The pitch method does not endorse speed and carelessness over relevance. Read all memos and documents completely. Before pitching a memorandum, ask if there is any concealed information in it that is valuable now or, more importantly, in the future.

As with businesses, athletic programs at all levels of competition become engulfed in mounds of paper. Memos, fliers, newsletters, and brochures are just a small number of items accumulating on our desks on a routine basis. There is an uncomplicated solution to this problem: It is called the pitch method. The pitch method is based on a three-step evaluation process. For example, when a departmental memo is generated and distributed to the program, a coach or program administrator can do one of three things: act on it, file it, or pitch it. If we originate our paper-flow thinking process with the third component (pitch it) first and work backwards, our offices would be less overrun with paper. If a memo or other item is meaningless (which half of them typically are), toss it and the problem is solved. If there is a piece of critical data in the document, there are two alternatives. It can be filed for future reference and subsequently thrown away when it becomes irrelevant, outdated, or obsolete, or it can be acted on by consolidating it into a list of things to do. It is that easy. The most significant consideration with this paper-flow technique is that the program does not amass piles of documents and papers. Simply address each document as soon as it arrives. This approach also has the beneficial side effect of timely responsiveness to all memos rather than accumulation and omission by fault.

Office Flow

The concept of office flow and workspace design is an exacting science that examines acoustics, lighting, safety, and temperature. To investigate the details of these highly specialized areas is beyond the scope of this text. However, office flow and design can be looked at strictly from an administrative perspective. In other words, how can we make our offices and work areas conducive to the best use of our time and effort? While their text was written for complex, massive office areas, the authors of the 1991 book *Planning and Designing the Office Environment* present a simple four-step, generalized-but-logical progression for examining work areas:

1. Define the administrative goals.
2. Carefully examine the current work area situation.
3. Establish a detailed set of user requirements.
4. Develop and implement solutions that fulfill these requirements.

Because most coaches and program administrators have departments that would be considered small by most business standards, the four-step evaluation process can be done in minutes. When defining the administrative goals, simply ask the following questions:

- What is the program's office(s) used for and what does it produce?
- Is record storage a priority?
- Is the office a meeting area?

The easiest way to tackle this problem is to make a list of all of the things created and accomplished in the office and prioritize that list. From there, examine the office's current operational status. Ask another basic question: Is the current office flow satisfying the program's office priorities? If not, document what user-requirements the office lacks and determine what would fulfill those requirements. The first step is probably the most overlooked in the process. Most administrators do not define what they want to produce from their work areas, so they really do not have them arranged very logically or effectively.

From there, there are only two other cardinal rules associated with office flow. The first provision is that *all of the actual work areas should be as far away from people traffic as possible.* The second is that *the work areas should be ordered and designed so that one can access everything in the office* (desks, files, fax) *while seated and on the phone.* If the coach or program administrator observes these two fundamental rules, the rest of the layout is up to personal disposition and usable space.

Computers

The final area of office organization is computers. There is only one requirement in regard to the use of computers in a coach's personal and professional life: Get one and learn to use it. Costs are rapidly declining, the

Administrative Tip

If the program's office is an area utilized for recruiting (either staff or athletes), stress the importance of a professional ambience. Obtain quality furniture within reasonable financial considerations. First impressions are usually the most powerful and, characteristically, endure the longest. Office atmosphere and class can communicate louder than words.

program workload can be cut in half, the operating systems and software are becoming increasingly user friendly, and the quantity of online data that can be utilized by the athletic program is increasing exponentially. The benefits far outweigh the costs.

In choosing the program's computer software, major considerations should be uniformity, consistency, and usability. It is strongly recommended that a popular, universally recognized, integrated software package be utilized. An integrated software program is one containing a word processor, spreadsheet, database, and presentation software. This all-inclusive package is not only cost effective, but also encompasses most, if not all, of the athletic program software needs. Currently, the most accepted and generally known integrated software package is Microsoft Office. This integrated package has numerous training courses associated with its use as well as abundant support literature. It has upgrading capabilities and should have a long software life.

Program Organization

The coach is the manager of the athletic program. To be successful, one should consider the program, no matter how large or small, a business. To think of it as anything else would be to restrict its capacity for expansion and ultimate success. From the management functional standpoint, planning is the initial and foremost priority in establishing the business. To recapitulate, planning is the future-oriented function of determining strategic goals for the program's operation. From this plan, the manager must mold and configure the enterprise to achieve the stated goals. This is the underlying thought behind organizational development and design.

Complexity, Formulation, Centralization

The principal considerations in organizing one's program should be for *structure* and *power*. In our context, *structure* involves a broad overview of our athletic programs (macro elements), while by *power* we refer to more specific aspects of our program (micro elements).

From the macrostructural perspective, there are three variables that are applicable to the study of sports programs:

Complexity: The extent to which the organization is divided into different divisions, departments, groups, and roles. Each component has its own tasks and responsibilities.

Formulation: The extent to which rules, regulations, job descriptions, and policies and procedures govern an organization.

Centralization: Refers to the level of hierarchical authority to make decisions. (Parkhouse, 1996)

For coaches, these three terms (*complexity*, *formulation*, and *centralization*) require program-encompassing thought about how and what we want to structure in our athletic program.

- *Complexity* should initiate questions such as How many different divisions or departments do we have? Are the divisions designed and structured for the maximum possible returns?
- *Formulation* refers to how rule-oriented our programs are. Do we have formal job descriptions? Do we have a policy and procedure document?
- Finally, *centralization* is simply who has (or should have) formal authority and power to make decisions.

From these three generalized concepts, we can begin to definitively organize our programs. While complexity and formulation are important elements to examine, the principal consideration in specifically organizing one's program is centralization or the notion of power.

Power and Authority

Power is defined as

> the capacity to affect organizational outcomes. From this simple doctrine, power can be broken down into two significant categories: internal influencers and external influencers. Internal influencers are full-time employees and staff who are charged with making decisions and taking actions on a permanent or regular basis; it is they who determine the outcomes of expressed goals pursued by the organization. The external influencers are nonemployees who use their basis of influence to affect the behavior of internal influencers (employees and staff) and to affect organizational outcomes. (Mintzberg, 1983)

Both internal and external influencers have substantial power and dominion over the productivity, quality, and success of the athletic programs they are associated with. As a manager of the athletic program, the coach or program administrator will need to shape and organize their powers to maximize performance.

As we scrutinize our operations, we need to distinguish those distinct individuals who are the program's internal and external influencers (other managerial theorists use the designation *stakeholder* instead of *influencer*). Internal influencers could include staff members, volunteers, athletes, parents' groups, etc. External influences might include athletic administrators, the board of directors of the program or school, other associated clubs and programs, and fan and supporter groups, among others.

Internal Influencers

Internal influencers are people over whom we, as the manager or coach, have sovereignty and control, including formal authority and legitimate power: "Legitimate power is the power and authority granted through the organization's hierarchical structure" (Griffin, 1990). The coach or program administrator is in the uppermost position of the internal organizational hierarchical diagram. This, in turn, gives the coach the explicit authority over internal influencers such as staff, managers, players,

Administrative Tip

When dealing with an individual's authority and influence, never forget that power is linked undeniably with people's egos. Be sensitive to the program stakeholders' personalities and egotistical composition. By no means should one ever disregard the potency of self-esteem and sense of worth. To overlook it would open a Pandora's box of personality conflicts.

and administrative assistants. How can one order and fashion the internal influencers so as to enhance their potential? Is it through the deftness and experience of the particular individual in the operation or is it through the importance of the operational functions of the position involved in achieving program goals? Emphatically stated: We should structure (or in some cases restructure) the organization on the basis of the functions of the positions rather than on the individuals in those positions. Does this mean that as the manager one should be utterly task oriented and disregard the human aspect of administration? No. It simply means that the tasks and responsibilities determine the program's infrastructure. People can come and go, but the significance of each job stays the same.

When internally structuring the program, there are four easy steps to follow:

1. Prioritize the factors for program success.
2. Model and configure them into job positions.
3. Classify those job positions into a hierarchical form.
4. Fill those positions with the most qualified people.

The counseling and motivating of individuals within each hierarchical position to pursue and achieve program objectives are a function of the coach's philosophy of human resource management and leadership (functions three and four in the management process).

Each internal position, from strictly a program viewpoint, needs a detailed and precise job description (see Appendix 3B). In this job description, list:

1. The official title of the position, summarizing its placement in the organization.
2. The functions of the position in order of the most significant to the least.
3. If feasible, an approximate range of time, in percentage form, of each function (50% of the position is recruiting, 25% is team training, etc.).
4. The empowerment of the position. In other words, the sanctioned authority delegated by the program coach/manager for the position.
5. The accountability of the position.
6. The reward system for the position.

After clarifying the program's internal power dispersal (through job descriptions), place each specific position in a conventional organizational chart, which maximizes its inherent power. "Organizational charts are diagrams that depict formal structure in programs. The typical chart shows various positions, the position holder, and the lines of authority linking them to one another" (Schermerhorn, 1988). The size of the internal organization will dictate the type of operational framework as well as its complexity.

The types of organizational structure theories in today's businesses are numerous. For our programs, an uncomplicated, classical method with direct lines of command is more than adequate. This traditional format (or vertical hierarchical chart) has distinct advantages even as it has some limitations. Its advantages include being a top-down blueprint that has clear lines of authority and communication, minimization of formal jurisdiction power struggles between different staff members, and the provision of status to primary areas necessary for program survival and prosperity. Its disadvantages include minimal coordination and interaction between non-aligned positions, lack of horizontal training (which promotes well rounded employees), potential for informal power friction between positions of the same level, and reduction of the ability of the staff to progress and advance in the program because all occupational promotions are on the vertical axis.

Organization should be a top priority for coaches and administrators. Staff members will perform better if they know the expectations of the job, their employment duties, the importance of the assignments in the hierarchical design, and their position's compensation and rewards. The documents (both job descriptions and hierarchical charts) should be readily accessible and always utilized in staff evaluations. Take time to create them. In the long run, it will save countless hours of miscommunication, supervision, and frustration. The aggregate total of all of the job descriptions should encompass every known element of the operation. Regard them as adaptable documents that can be molded to fit the program's needs if the situational environment changes.

External Influencers

External influencers are people who have a stake in the business or program and have formal or informal authority over the program. One's first impression after reading the previous statement is, "How can a coach or program administrator have organizational control over people who have power or jurisdiction over the program and its operation?" There are two solutions:

1. Pleasant avoidance.
2. Aggressive incorporation.

Pleasant avoidance is almost self explanatory: Endeavor to make the program as self-sufficient as at all possible and evade/avoid (pleasantly) external influencers. This is also known as diffusing external influencers' power. In predicaments of conflict and confrontation with the external influencer, promptly and calmly resolve the problem or requirement and proceed with the program's regular operations. In some circumstances, this might be the only technique for organizing and dealing with incompatible and demanding external influencers. Fulfill all requirements requested and stay away from that individual. The chief advantage of this technique is less trepidation, aggravation, and stress for everyone involved in the operation (internal influencers). The disadvantage is the loss of a potential program patron and supporter.

The second program tactic involves aggressively incorporating the external influencer into the organization's family. In other words, the coach or program administrator's management obligation is to develop and organize a continuous public relations plan that summons people of influence

Administrative Tip

An imperative key in dealing with external influencers is perceptive empathy. An insensitive act (even unintentionally) could do enormous damage to the support structure of the program. Try to know the program's influencers and anticipate their possible reactions to certain situations.

and power into the program. The danger is evident: Once inside the organizational structure, without tactical supervision and control, these individuals could use their power to bring about internal disorder and destruction.

To organize the external influencer, reverse the fundamental thought of internal influencers. Remember, to structure the internal influencers, look at the function of the position over the individual. For external influencers, prioritize and structure the individuals and what they require and want out of the program. Make an inventory of external stakeholders and develop particular listings of each of their expectations, requirements, and agendas. At that point, have a systematic game plan for providing each one with generalized data in a timely manner. The benefits from this are plentiful. The external influencer will perceive that he or she has a vested interest in the program and will then use resources and capabilities to improve and help the athletic program.

Summary

Both personal and professional program organization are essential operational components for successful athletic programs. Through organization, one can reasonably employ all personal and program resources to the program's mission and its achievement of operational goals. The program will be able to effectively utilize personal and program power as well as control and develop external patrons and followers. A properly ordered professional environment can do several positive things:

1. Convey professionalism that, in turn, inspires confidence.
2. Minimize stakeholder and influencer apprehension about the operation and about their specific roles.
3. Provide a competitive edge in the arena by furnishing the coaches, staff, and players more time to concentrate efforts on improving skills and capabilities in their particular fields rather than catching up on a disorganized workload.

Chapter 3 ....

Human Resource Management

Objectives

- To define human resource practices used by contemporary businesses and apply those techniques to athletic programs.
- To present an understanding of staffing systems as they relate to tracking demand shifts, manpower planning, and recruiting concepts.
- To explain the five-stage selection process as it relates to athletics.
- To explore concepts of human resource training and development.
- To clarify human resource evaluations (MBOs).
- To review the fundamentals of athletic program compensation and benefits.

Introduction

Human resource management "is the process of ensuring that employees are selected, developed, and rewarded for accomplishing goals" (Bedeian, 1993). In other words, human resource administration is a hands-on, people-oriented function. It directly correlates to the productivity of the program. Productivity can be thought of as the acquisition and effective utilization of resources to maximize organizational worth. Undoubtedly, the most indispensable resources in any program or business are its human resources.

This chapter highlights the managerial component of human resource planning and management. Because these principles are generically applicable to all businesses, situations, and industries, they can freely be adapted and applied to athletic programs. Inside a particular athletic program, the two sources of human resources: 1. program staff (coaches, secretaries,

Administrative Tip

Never disregard the crucial reality that the people in one's organization are the lifeblood of productivity. A coach or program administrator could never achieve any of the program's goals if it was not for their dedication and hard work. Consciously focus on the concept of lifeblood of productivity when dealing with the program's most valuable resource: its people.

managers, volunteers, etc., and 2. athletes. The following tactics can be utilized throughout program operations to support these two internal stakeholder groups.

Human Systems in Athletic Organizations

In today's business world, organizational philosophies and obligations toward the human element have gone beyond the simple duties of hiring, firing, and filling gaps. Modern human resource management systems embrace concepts such as employee enhancement and satisfaction, increased productivity though empowerment, and providing social environments for long-term commitment. This new perspective on developing and maximizing human potential should be a part of each athletic program's agenda and operation. Coaches need to perceive that each program (no matter what the extent or competitive level) is a business and that staff members and players are employee stakeholders. If coaches, as the program administrators, commit to this basic premise, they will need to construct a system that comprises four vital human resource operations:

- Staffing—recruitment, selection, and placement.
- Training and Development—training activities, counseling, and career planning.
- Evaluations—joint analysis of performance expectations and accomplishments.
- Compensation—wages, performance incentives, and miscellaneous benefits.

Staffing Systems

From the standpoint of athletic administration, a coach's skillful use of staffing systems is related to acquiring the precise number and the highest qualified staff and athletes. This segment analyzes the human resource concepts of demand shift analysis, manpower planning, and recruitment and selection.

Demand Shift Analysis

When initiating a discussion on staffing, one must first examine the internal organizational demand for human resources and the factors that affect that demand. In the 1989 text *Human Resources and Personnel Management*, Werther and Davis identify three major elements that might

---

Figure 1: Demand Shift Factors for Personnel (Werther and Davis, 1989)

External	Organizational	Workforce
Economic	Strategic Plan	Retirement
Social/Political/Legal	Budgets	Resignation
Technological	New Ventures	Termination
Competitors	Organizational Job Design	LOAs

shift (increase or decrease) an athletic program's demand for staff and athletes. Figure 1 is an adaptation of their concept.

The external components (economic, social/political/legal, technological, competitive) are factors that need to be examined and tracked continuously to see if they are affecting or will affect the future of a program.

External environmental questions:

- How will a fundamental shift in our local, regional, or national economic condition affect our program? Since athletic programs rely on disposable income for funding (either through paid attendance or donations), will an economic change in our operating community result in a financial change in our internal operating system? In turn, will this shift our financial situation, affecting our staff?
- How do EEOC, Affirmative Action, Disabilities Act, and other governmental regulations affect us? Is our program considered socially responsible in its staffing and athletic recruitment? What does our governing athletic association state about staffing and athletic recruitment?
- Will we be able to increase our program's staffing and operations through effective use of technology?
- What are our competitors doing in terms of staffing and athletic recruitment? Are they growing or downsizing? Are they focusing their human resource efforts on a certain individual with particular strengths and areas of expertise?

These are just a few of the questions that could be asked when examining the external factors that can affect a program's staffing demands. It should be noted that whenever one is examining any external environmental element that could affect an athletic program (not only from a human resource perspective, but from the perspectives of all areas of operation), look at each factor as an opportunity or a threat. If it is an opportunity, strategize how to exploit it. If the environmental element is a threat, minimize it.

Internal elements that might shift a program's demand for human resources are *organizational forces* and *workforce*. These internal factors need continuous oversight and management. Organizational elements such as a program's strategic plan, budget and forecasted projections, new ventures, and job designs are all explicit documents that have a direct relationship to human resource needs. According to Werther and Davis

> major organizational decisions affect the demand for human resources. The organization's strategic plan is most influential on H.R. decision. It commits the program to long range objectives—such as growth, new products, markets, or services. These objectives dictate the number and type of employees needed in the future. If long-term objectives are to be met, develop long range human resource plans that accommodate the strategic plan. (Werther and Davis, 1989)

Administrative Tip

The program's size will determine its demand shift analysis. Obviously, the smaller the staff and athlete base, the less analytical thought and structure need go into a demand shift analysis. Conversely, the smaller the staff and athlete foundation, the more important replacement becomes.

Budgeting and forecasting (which will be covered in later chapters) are the most obvious and immediate determinants for staffing and players. Budgeting and forecasting delineate and place into focus what an organization can spend fiscally and what it projects to spend and earn in the future. They determine the program's size, operational limits, equipment and facilities, and human resource limitations.

Another organizational planned strategy is *new ventures*. If planned properly, not only will these ventures have goals and structure, but they will also have human resource demands within specific timeframes. New ventures are directly related to the program plan and should be included with that document.

The last of the internal organizational elements that affect human resource demand is *job design*. Job design refers to the initial development of positions in a new venture or the restructuring of positions in an ongoing operation. Either way, new job designs and descriptions typically mean a fundamental change in internal human resource demand.

The second internal element that might shift human resource demand is the program's *current workforce*. Coaches and program administrators should see the program's staff and players as a workforce. This workforce must be thought of as a flexible, flowing component of an operation that could change daily. Some changes can be anticipated in advance and planned for, such as, for example, a scheduled retirement or an anticipated leave of absence. However, other changes might not be so easy to predict. Sudden and critical demand can arise from resignation, employment termination, or severe illness and injury. To compensate for abrupt shifts in a program's human resource demands, a program will need to have in place a well defined staffing system.

Once a need for human resources has determined through staff and player demand analysis, a coach or program administrator must apply a systematic staffing strategy. Staffing strategies for athletic programs (for either players or staff members) can be isolated into three types: manpower planning, recruiting, selection.

Manpower Planning

Manpower planning (which is similar to human resource demand forecasting but more specific and narrowly defined) is

> the process of 1. forecasting the needs of the program over some future time period for added human resources; 2. surveying the pool of skills currently available among the programs employees and players as well as in the job markets and recruitable player ranks; 3. deciding on ways to meet the needs of the program. (Peterson, 1979)

From a staff outlook, the manager needs to carefully analyze both long-term goals, which are future-oriented by nature, and short-term objectives, which call for more immediate actions. One must prioritize which of these goals (short and action-oriented or long and future-oriented) are critical and in need of quality staff members or players. Two scenarios may emerge

Administrative Tip

Depth charts can have two valuable purposes in an athletic program. The first and most evident is that they evaluate the functional turnover of the program. The second is that they can be used as motivational tools. Some staff members and athletes might not be content with where they lie in the program's depth chart. This could encourage them to increase their tangible productivity levels as well as intensify their intangible commitment to the program.

from this process. The first is that the existing manpower position is deemed sufficient for the program's future goals and direction. In this case, the administrator or coach might need to do some adjusting of job responsibilities and workloads, but the staff and athletes will remain essentially the same. The second scenario is that the program's manpower needs are deemed insufficient and will require additional staffing to attain the future program projections.

The one inherent constant in all athletic programs is that there will always be player turnover. Turnover can come from age limitations, graduation, quitting, injury, or other situations. Manpower planning for athletic programs can be accomplished simply through a diagram known as a depth chart. A depth chart is a versatile diagram that lists the positions in the program and the people in each position. How the coach delineates and designs the graph is entirely subjective. One possible design is as follows:

1. Across the topmost section of the chart, list the positions in the program or on the team.
2. Arrange the program players under each category in order of significance and value. If there are players who are multiskilled, classify and index them under their primary area.
3. After placing players in descending order, color code them for age, grade, or other critical criteria. For example, in a college setting, all seniors could be highlighted in one color, juniors in another, and so forth.

This diagram will furnish the coach a visual picture of future recruiting requirements as or well as or where each player is currently situated in the program. Always consider this document a flexible chart. Players can progress up and (unfortunately) down as their abilities increase or decrease.

Recruiting and Selection

After manpower planning assessments have been outlined and there is a definite internal human resource need, the next logical procedure in staffing is recruiting. "Recruiting consists of activities intended to identify sources of talent to meet program needs and to attract the right number and types of people for the right jobs at the right time and in the right place" (Rothwell, 1988). Recruiting sources for athletic staff members can include media advertising, networking, and internal referencing. Recruiting sources for players can come from many areas depending on the program's level of play, funding, and networking capacity. For example, college recruiting can come from high schools, junior elite programs, foreign contacts, grapevines, etc. Often the program's financial circumstances will determine which recruiting sources to utilize.

Now that the sources have been clarified, the next stage is the selection process. The selection process (which can be terminated at any time) customarily proceeds as follows:

Phase One: Phase one consists of an informal preliminary evaluation. In other words, it is the assessment of the talent of a potential staff member or athlete. It can be as informal as the program manager and other

Administrative Tip

Before conducting a face-to-face dialogue with a prospective staff member or athlete, prepare a list of appropriate questions that will prioritize vital information needed to evaluate the candidate. Outline the presentation, but encourage open dialog. Keep in mind that the more one is practiced at interviewing, the better one will become at it. Another critical aspect of interviewing is to avoid letting the conversation go too far out on tangential topics. These interviewing digressions will lead the conversations to irrelevant subjects instead of program operations and the interviewee's fit within those operations.

staff members verbally assessing a candidate's qualifications or as formal as charting detailed selection criteria and quantifying the results.

Phase Two: Phase two consists of applications and questionnaires. These two instruments are accepted and recognized techniques for gathering pertinent information regarding a specific individual. The design of these instruments is limited by legal boundaries. For staff members, employment applications must conform with all Equal Employment Opportunity Commission and Privacy Information Act provisos and stipulations. Milkovich and Boudreau support this by saying

> though Title VII of the civil rights act does not specifically prohibit particular types of questions, asking questions that might be used to reject projected groups (such as gender, marital status, religion) is risky. . . many organizations simply refrain from asking such questions. (1991)

Player questionnaires are characteristically legislated by the governing body under which the program operates (NCAA, NAIA, high school, etc.).

Phase Three: Phase three consists of face-to-face conferences. Coaches and program administrators initiate this meeting through a conventional interview process. The intensity and format of the interview is determined by the significance and gravity of the position in the organization's operating scheme. Athlete face-to-face meetings can be home visits, campus visits, program meetings, individual counseling, etc. Once again, the controlling athletic association will determine the composition and duration of the encounters. Additionally, throughout this phase, contacting players in the form of written correspondence as well as additional evaluations is advisable.

Phase Four: Phase four consists of reference checks. This step in the selection process is habitually disregarded, but is crucial in affirming the character of the staff member or player. The coach or program administrator should have a slate of definite questions ready for all reference communications.

Phase Five: Phase five consists of negotiations and hiring or acquisition. After all the germane information has been assembled and references checked, the decision is made to offer the position. There are two consequential rules that must always be applied whether securing additional staff members or recruiting players. The first standard is to always convey the truth in all recruiting practices no matter how much the program might desire or need a particular individual. The second is to never "negative recruit" against another organization for a staff member or player. Negative recruiting is basically identifying other competitors for a potential staff member or athletic recruit and verbalizing derogatory remarks about their program, coaching methodology, and overall organization. Violating these basic rules will always come back to haunt the program one is trying to build or maintain.

Training and Development

The one competency on which all coaches concentrate is the training of techniques and skills. It is the teaching aspect of the profession that most coaches enjoy. Training and development augment the program's most valuable resource: people. There is a wealth of instructional methodologies that a coach can utilize. However, no matter what the sport, level of athlete, area of participation, or complexity of design, "there are three universal forms of training that circumvent all boundaries: skill training, knowledge training, and attitude training" (Steinmetz and Todd, 1986).

Skill Training

Skill training is the refining of specific dexterities and corporal abilities. In the coaching of athletics, this equates to instructing the physical portion of sports. Skill instruction can take on various forms. Two primary methods are *block training* and *random training*.

Block training is teaching skills through the unremitting repetition of a particular movement or activity. Simply put, the movement is completed over and over again until it is proficiently and adeptly displayed. It should be noted that there are no set number of repetitions to achieve competency. Human beings learn at disparate rates. As a coach, recognize this fact and, through pragmatic observation and distinct evaluation, analyze each person's progress accordingly.

Random instruction is the teaching of a particular skill or action through game-like situations and competitive activities. In random training, the exercises, drills, and teaching techniques are scenario driven, which means that the game or competitive condition is defined specifically for the individual(s), then the activity is conducted in a contest-like, live-action state. Random training has some distinctive advantages in its application. Some of the benefits:

1. It is as close to real-world competition as training can be.
2. It has participative learning in unsystematic conditions.
3. It combines the whole of the skill or activity rather than block training, which trains parts to make the whole.
4. It has the capacity to be dynamic and can keep the athletes' cognitive focus longer.

Knowledge Training

Knowledge training guides and teaches an individual to think. Knowledge training in athletics is as individual as each sport. The range of knowledge instruction can go from the basic Xs and Os to complex strategizing and conditional analysis. The concept of intelligence training and development encompasses business and psychological theories such as individual cognitive analysis, preconditions of learning (acceptance and motivation), creative cognitions, and rationality among others.

Administrative Tip

Before a negotiation of any kind, evaluate which elements are negotiable and which are not. Have the attitude that negotiations, by their very nature, are accommodating interactions. However, you need to declare up front which items in the meeting are open for discussion and which items are 'deal breakers'. Not only will you avoid critical personnel errors by using this technique, you will set the tempo of the interview and have total control of the negotiations.

Administrative Tip

No matter what type of training is being performed (skill, knowledge, attitudinal), never undervalue the influence of fun. The more a coach or program administrator can balance training goals with a pleasurable environment, the more productive the training sessions will be.

Administrative Tip

Whether one is block training (repetition training) or random training (real-life training), make sure new learning is programmed as early as practical in the training session. New learning takes a focused concentration, which is easier for the learner at the outset of a training session when he or she is fresh.

Take into account when discussing and training attitudes that idiosyncratic personalities are involved. Any time personalities are scrutinized and discussed, as a leader, mentally emphasize understanding and empathy for the individual involved in the training. Special note: Each person handles attitudinal instruction and debate differently. Spend time appreciating the human being and his or her reactions before embarking on attitudinal training.

Attitudinal Training

Attitudinal training is concerned with the character, disposition, and mindset of an individual. This is by far the most difficult type of training for the obvious reason that attitudes are immeasurable and from an individual perspective. However, there is way that we, as leaders, can instruct our staff and players on attitudinal expectations.

1. Candidly discuss what attitudes are anticipated and expected.
2. Document the behaviors and attitudes projected so each individual has a tangible reference.
3. Lead by example.

The third component could be the most potent of the three. If a coach or program administrator displays an impoverished, pessimistic, and unenthusiastic attitude, then his or her players and staff will more than likely adopt the same stance. Conversely, if a coach or program administrator exhibits an encouraging, optimistic attitude, the staff and athletes can observe, reference, and follow that behavior.

No matter what type of training (skill, knowledge, attitudinal), the instruction of a program's personnel (staff and players) can also be systematized for more consistent and competent results. William McGhee, in his 1977 publication, *Training and Developing Theory: Policies and Practices*, conceptualizes a successive four-step process for training and development. The following is an adaptation of his process as it applies to athletic programs.

Step 1: For each staff member and team player, the coach should do a deficiency evaluation to accentuate individual areas that demand improvment. This stage is also known as a skills inventory.

Step 2: For each staff member and player, the coach needs to outline a particular course of action that describes strategies and objectives to enhance the individual's abilities.

Crain states that training objectives and tactics should follow guidelines:

1. Personal training goals and program objectives must be compatible.
2. Training objectives must be realistic.
3. Training objectives must be clearly communicated.
4. Targeted results must be measurable and verifiable. (1986)

Step 3: The third step is the implementation and execution of training regimens.

Step 4: The final step is the evaluation of the program's training system (Steps 1-3). This inspection audit compares verifiable outcomes against forecasted training aspirations. Two items require emphasis. First, when at all possible, quantify results when dealing with skill and knowledge training systems. Additionally, since attitudinal training is qualitative in nature (its measurement is by subjective opinion), gather more than one person's opinion on attitudinal changes. Second, if there is an unfavorable deviation from projected to actual results, the system should be redesigned to remedy the training deficiencies. Positive deviations and improvements in which the results exceed forecasted projections should also be examined and used to fortify any future staff or athlete training.

Evaluations

The primary intention behind the evaluation of a program's staff and its players' productivity is to supply feedback to internal stakeholders, to standardize goals, and to improve productivity outcomes. There are abundant methodologies that can be employed when completing performance evaluations. One of the most contemporary practices for evaluating employees is based on the concept of management by objective appraisals (MBOs).

MBO assessments are a more cooperative, motivational, and constructive method of staff and player evaluation than the traditional one-way critical judgment analysis.

Management by objectives is a system that features an agreement by a superior and a subordinate on the subordinate's objectives for a particular period and a periodic review of how well the subordinate achieved those objectives. MBO systems generally include the following steps:

1. The supervisor and subordinate mutually agree on the primary elements of the subordinate's position.
2. The supervisor and subordinate mutually agree on the subordinate's specific objectives for the specific period.
3. The subordinate (with assistance from the supervisor) establishes a plan of action necessary to meet each objective.
4. During the specific period, the subordinate periodically reviews progress toward objectives, perhaps jointly with the supervisor. Progress checks may indicate that there is a need to change the action plan (step 3) or modify objectives (step 2).
5. At the end of the specific period, the supervisor and subordinate meet to mutually evaluate the prior performance objectives verses the actual results. (French, 1994)

This process is a perpetual and repeating system. From the five-step process, a key term must be emphasized: *mutual.* This collaborative type of evaluation process is in the best interest of the staff member, the athlete, and the program. From the vantage point of the athlete or staff, the system is good because it supports individuals with clear objectives that have been established with their own input. Furthermore, coaches will find that this method bolsters staff and player confidence and levels of motivation, creates strong lines of communication, and cultivates teamwork.

Two other key points should be emphasized in employing MBO evaluations. Remember that evaluations are a collaborative effort. At first, the coach might have to "draw out" the player or staff member in the partnership aspects of clarifying objectives. It should also be clear that the player or staff member is accountable for his or her performance. The second key

Administrative Tip

Whatever evaluation technique utilized, when assessing and commenting on a staff member or athlete's shortcomings and inadequacies, always start off the criticism with a sincere positive comment about a constructive action that the subordinate has contributed to the program. From there, discuss the area that needs improvement. The reason to start with a positive comment is to keep the staff member or athlete in the right frame of mind. A positive mindset is receptive, while a negative mindset is blocked.

Administrative Tip

Often the most difficult aspects of an MBO evaluation is drawing out the staff member or athlete to contribute to the process. To have them collaborate in their own productivity and future, uncover what motivates them. Start the MBO process there in order to get them vested in all aspects of their position. Explain to them the critical importance of items that might not be individual motivators.

point is that there should be intermittent checkpoints throughout the time period. These checkpoints can be in the form of formal meetings or informal updates.

Compensation and Benefits

The final human resource system in the program relates to the compensation and benefit packages proposed to potential and current staff members and players.

Compensation systems can influence

1. Who is attracted to the organization as well as who remains.
2. The level of employee motivation and promotion of equity.
3. The overall climate and culture of the organization.
4. The overall organizational structure.
5. The level of operating costs. (Butler, 1991)

Contrary to the three previous human systems (staffing, training, evaluations), compensation in coaching and playing arenas will be determined by the rules regarding professionalism. Staff members, however, can qualify for the same compensation rewards as any other business employee. Their compensations, awards, and benefits can include salaries or wages, commissions, performance bonuses, vacation and sick leave, pension and retirement, profit sharing, and workmen's compensation. The level and detail of the program's employee compensation package is dictated by the operational environment and the specific situation.

If an individual has the opportunity to coach athletes in a professional setting, the above employee criteria for compensation would apply. However, a majority of coaches are bound by the rules of amateurism and the sport's governing organization, under which compensation is strictly controlled. Colleges have a compensation system supported by scholarships. The governing organization's (NCAA, NAIA, NJCAA, etc.) have determined a very detailed set of rules regarding scholarships. Junior Olympic levels and high school programs are also strictly bound by the rules of amateurism.

Summary

For a business (in this case athletic program) to be prosperous, one truth must pervade the organization's philosophy and thinking: The program is only as good as the people in it. The selection, training, evaluation, and compensation of a program's staff and athletes have an absolute and unequivocal impact on all aspects of the program. The competent utilization of human resource applications can fortify this imperative resource. The deficiency of human resource management can spell complete failure.

APPENDIX 3A: Human Resource Disciplinary Systems

The following is an escalating, stage-by-stage disciplinary system for athletic programs.

Stage 1: Oral/Verbal Warnings

Level 1: Oral/Verbal Warning (No Documentation)
This form of warning is for lesser/minor program offenses. No followup or written documentation is associated with this type of warning.

Level 2: Oral/Verbal Warning (Documentation)
This disciplinary discussion warrants some manner of supporting written documentation for referencing. It should be kept as a permanent record in the staff/athlete program file.

Stage 2: Written Warnings

Level 1: Written Warning (Internal Documentation)
This phase and intensity of disciplinary action has a formal, signed form retained in the staff/athlete's program file. It should be discussed at an official meeting with other program members in attendance. All who participate (including the violator) should sign off on the document.

Level 2: Written Warning (Internal and External Documentation)
The subsequent level of a response is the same as Level 1 except that the written portion is maintained not only inside the player's program file, but also in the overall organization's and department's operation records. Because of the gravity of this violation, it is advisable to have a departmental administrator present to observe the meeting.

Stage 3: Suspensions/Dismissals

Level 1: Suspensions
This critical disciplinary situation involves the staff member/athlete receiving a participative suspension from all program activities. The length of the suspension could be predetermined or could be set through an advisory meeting with the organization's administration. All suspensions must be entirely documented with the full knowledge and support of all organizational administrators. The athlete/staff member can bring in outside counsel if so desired.

Level 2: Dismissal
This terminal stage involves the staff member/athlete's permanent discharge/release from all program activities and functions. Because of the definitive severity of this type of response to an infringement/violation, all parties should be well represented. Once again, comprehensive documentation is mandatory. It is also prudent to video tape the dismissal conference.

A few salient points about the workings of the system: Continued offenses move up the stage by stage process. Major offenses skip the lower levels of disciplinary actions. Define, in writing, typical (and if possible specific) offenses in each category and level. Provide all staff/athletes with a copy of the disciplinary system and discuss it with them periodically.

APPENDIX 3B: Construction of a Job Description

The following layout is the underlying structure of a job description. This design can be easily modified to fit all types of athletic programs. The detail in each job description will be influenced by the complexity of the organization and the intricacy of the position.

Job Title

The first division of the job description is the formal and specialized name for the position in the organization. Other information in this section:
- Job number.
- Operational division.
- Creation date of job description.
- Position in hierarchal scheme—accountability and reporting responsibilities.
- Salary range and compensation package associated with the position.

Occupational Overview

This is the narrative synopsis of the position and its practical importance in the program. While broad in scope, it should give the reader a sense also of the details associated with the position.

Job Specifications

The job specifications portion of a job description is a delineation of the primary activities involved in the position. It is advisable to do the following:
- Put all tasks, responsibilities, and functions in priority order.
- Bullet tasks, responsibilities, and functions for clarity.
- If possible, place estimated percentages of time for each task, responsibility, and function as they relate to the overall position.

Knowledge and Ability Requirements for the Position

This segment stipulates the mental and physical aspects mandated to execute the position. Educational minimums, size and weight requirements, and diverse prior job experience are all components of this part.

APPENDIX 3C: Job Instruction Training Procedures

In their 1999 textbook, *Human Resource Management*, Fisher, Schoenfeldt, and Shaw devise a two-phase process for job instruction. The following display can be easily customized to all sports programs.

Phase 1: Get Ready to Instruct

1. Have a timetable.
   —How much skill is expected and when.
2. Break down the job.
   —List the important steps.
   —Pick out the key points.
3. Have everything ready.
   —The right equipment, materials, and supplies.
4. Have the workplace properly arranged.
   —As one would expect the worker to maintain it.

Phase 2: How to Instruct

1. Prepare the worker.
   —Put the worker at ease.
   —Find out what he/she knows.
   —Arouse interest.
   —Place the worker correctly.
2. Present the operation.
   —Tell.
   —Show.
   —Explain.
   —Demonstrate.
3. Try out performance.
   —Have the worker perform the operation.
   —Have the worker explain the key points.
   —Correct the errors.
   —Re-instruct as needed.
4. Follow up.
   —Put the worker on his or her own.
   —Encourage questions.
   —Check frequently.
   —Taper off assistance.

Chapter 4 ....
Leadership

Objectives

- To present the breadth of conceptual definitions for leadership.
- To stress leadership's commitment and obligation to total quality management.
- To identify inept listening tendencies and behaviors.
- To impart effective listening habits.
- To account for nonverbal communication as it relates to leadership.
- To examine various factors of situational leadership.

Introduction

This section examines the dynamic subject of leadership. The chapter investigates conceptual definitions as well as historical and contemporary concepts of leadership such as communication, listening, and situational leadership. All aspects of business and group leadership are related to the function of coaching and program administration. The chapter concludes with appendix components that highlight numerous theories of leadership and leadership approaches as well as the communication process for leaders.

Conceptual Definitions

The sheer volume of modern literature devoted to the subject of leadership is staggering. In today's business world, leadership is the one dominant characteristic that every organization is trying to identify, cultivate, and retain. It is a subject that has evolved from a single basic concept to one with elaborate models and theoretical definitions. Historically, the classic concept of leadership related to an individual's formal power, which is inherent in the organizational structure. The hierarchical, vertical chain-of-command structure has one person answering directly to or following orders from a

Administrative Tip

It is essential for a coach or program administrator to know one's own leadership style, personality, and abilities. There are countless personality tests available that are both reliable and valid. If possible, self-administer at least three personality/leadership tests to expose one's approach to leadership. Be truthful in all of the answers. Compile the results into a personality/leadership profile.

superior. The modern concept of leadership has authority but goes well beyond this to encompass motivation, communication, and situational analysis, among others.

Before defining modern leadership, one must determine the factors that should be present for leadership to emerge. There are three conspicuous ingredients that must be present for leadership to emerge. First and most evident, a leader must have subordinates or followers (staff and athletes). Secondly, he or she must have a foundation of applicable power and authority to assert, influence, and control subordinates. Finally, a leader must have a purpose or mission toward which to lead or maneuver the group. As coaches, we maneuver our programs under these three stipulations. In other words, we have the situation and environment for leadership.

The difficulty intrinsic to leadership is that there is no generally accepted definition. It is a dynamic subject that is as diverse as each of us. The following definitions give us a range of insights into the term leadership. In the 1988 book, *The Leadership Factor*, John Kotter defines leadership as the process of moving groups of people in some direction through (mostly) noncoercive means. . . leadership moves people in a direction that is generally in their long-term best interest.

Manz and Sims in their 1989 book, *Super Leadership,* see the concept of leadership as having two elements. Self-leadership is an extensive set of strategies focused on the behaviors and thoughts that people use to influence themselves. A super leader is one who leads others to lead themselves. A super leader designs and implements the system that allows and teaches employees to be self-leaders.

Another concept of leadership comes from Hackman and Johnson's 1991 book, *Leadership: A Communication Perspective*. It defines leadership as a human (symbolic) communication that modifies the attitudes and behaviors of others in order to meet group goals and needs.

As one can observe from just these three examples, there are abundant definitions for leadership: all different, yet all correct in their own way (or context). The next logical question: To which one do I subscribe? Simply put, all of them apply at one time or another. This is the basic premise behind the concept of situational leadership, which will be examined at the end of this chapter.

Leadership Commitment to Quality

It is well documented throughout thousands of managerial texts and writings that the single most important philosophy in today's business world relates to leadership's/management's commitment to the concept of total quality management (TQM). In beginning any discussion of leadership, the element of commitment to quality should be the first and foremost consideration. This concept (originated by Edward Deming) emphasizes that every action in an organization (in our case, team and program) should have quality as its primary objective. In other words, TQM can be adopted, implemented, and continually enhanced by our athletic programs.

What exactly is total quality management and how can we as coaches (through our team leadership) utilize these principles in our athletic programs? Edward Deming, who was one of the most influential business figures of the 20th century, created a 14-point philosophy on quality management that is universal to all businesses. The following is a summary of his philosophy as it relates to athletic programs and coaching leadership (adapted from Kreitner, 1995).

1. Constant purpose—Strive for continuous improvement and quality in all aspects of the program to stay competitive.
2. New philosophy—Demand wiser use of limited resources.
3. Give up on quality inspections—If quality is built in from the beginning, inspection should be unnecessary.
4. Avoid the constant search for the lowest costs.
5. Seek continuous improvements—Constantly improve operational processes for greater productivity and lower use of resources and time.
6. Train everyone—Make sure each staff member or athlete has a clear idea how to do his or her job.
7. Provide real leadership—Leading is more than simply telling. . . provide individual assistance to everyone in program.
8. Drive fear out of the workplace—Staff and athletes are going to continue to do things wrong when they are afraid to ask questions about how and why.
9. Promote teamwork—Keep common goals.
10. Avoid slogans—Provide leadership and continually improve the system and the results will take care of themselves.
11. Get rid of quotas—When staff members and athletes aggressively pursue individual quotas and statistics, they lose sight of quality.
12. Remove barriers that stifle pride in development and performance.
13. Education and self-improvement are the key. . . greater knowledge means greater opportunities.
14. Quality is everyone's job and responsibility.

How does a program leader develop these philosophies of quality? Elements such as individual style and persona, communication, and the current situational factors are all critical. However, the first step is to develop an environment that makes quality a priority by doing the following:

1. Develop relationships of openness and trust.
2. Build collaboration and teamwork.
3. Manage and lead by fact.
4. Support results in quality through recognition and reward.
5. Stress continuous improvement and learning. (Schmidt and Finnigan, 1993)

Without providing these elements, quality will be de-emphasized and the outcomes will be diminished. Additionally, the above environmental factors lead to quality and enhanced performance, which, in turn, leads to

Administrative Tip

Quality should be pictured as an upward-flowing model, which goes from small actions to large program outcomes. If a coach or program administrator can instill quality in every action and thought that program members take (no matter how small the deed may be), then the overall program quality will already be in place. Minor actions combine to produce significant results.

the next definitive question: How does the coach or program administrator provide this type of cooperative, goal-oriented, progressive-feeling environment? The two factors that are critical to determining success are one's communication and listening style and the situational leadership approach.

Leadership Communication—Listening

Being an effective communicator is essential to being a competent leader. Being able to impart critical information and to guide people charismatically is typically the initial characteristic that people associate with leadership communication. The other side, which is perhaps the most overlooked and neglected skill of leadership, is proactive listening. For a program's success, active listening to staff and athletes is often a more critical function of leadership than being a great speaker. Proactive listening can rejuvenate interpersonal exchanges, gather imperative information for decision-making, and function as a prerequisite for productivity and rewards.

Ineffectual Listening Habits

There can be many causes of ineffectual listening. Regardless of whether the barriers to competent listening are environmental, physiological, or psychological, the identification and intentional elimination of these blockades is critical. Factors of improper and defective listening can encompass:

1. Fact-listening: Dissecting messages only for facts, not intended meanings and denotations.
2. Thinking of an argument: Instead of listening and concentrating on the message, a poor listener diverts his or her attention to rebuttals and counterattacks.
3. Being critical of semantics: Being narrowly focused on semantic (meaning of words) misinterpretations and misuses and concentrating on the technical instrument of communication rather than the themes and ideas being communicated.
4. Dissecting delivery: Focusing attention on the method of delivery (the how) rather than the substance and content of information transmitted (the what).
5. Frozen evaluation: Having a negative preconception of a message and/or speaker will repress information being communicated.
6. Pretending to listen: Faking alertness.
7. Taking detailed notes: Taking and transcribing notes obsessively is detrimental to comprehension because meanings and nuances are lost.
8. Rushing communication: Impatient and often self-centered rushing of the speaker maintains an apathetic, nonconducive communication environment.
9. Hearing, not listening: Hearing and listening are overlapping but different concepts. Hearing is the physical registration of sounds,

Administrative Tip

To become mindful of ineffectual listening habits, consciously observe as many conversations as possible and look for clues of impending communication breakdowns. From those witnessed communication failures, one can become cognizant of one's own conversations and ineffectual habits.

while listening is the reception, comprehension, and assimilation of information.

10. Daydreaming: Self explanatory.

Effective Listening Habits

In his 1986 publication titled *Handbook of Executive Communication*, John DiGaetani expounds on 11 supplementary characteristics of an effective listener. There are certain characteristics that designate good listening and these are characteristics a good leader should strive to possess:

1. Looks at the subordinate when speaking and listening.
2. Questions the subordinate to clarify what was said.
3. Shows concern by asking questions about the subordinate's feelings.
4. Repeats points made by the subordinate.
5. Does not rush the subordinate.
6. Is poised and emotionally controlled.
7. Responds with a nod of the head and smiles.
8. Pays close attention.
9. Keeps on the subject until the subordinate competes his/her thoughts.
10. Does not interrupt the subordinate.
11. Maintains a positive attitude by conveying an honest concern.

Nonverbal Listening

There is another area of listening that does not require verbal interpretation. For a coach to become an even more effective listener-leader, he or she needs to be a decoder of nonverbal communication. How can a coach become an adept observer of nonverbal communication? First and most significantly, an effective leader realizes that nonverbal behaviors are situational and personalized. "The specific situation, environment, time factor, cultural background, and personal frame of reference must all be considered. Not every nonverbal behavior means exactly the same thing in all situations" (Hamilton and Parker, 1982). Secondly, deft communicators suppress their own subjective presumptions and feelings while evaluating and interpreting kinetics (body language). Finally, all versatile leaders dissect and notice facial expressions and eye movement. "Researchers have estimated that the human face is capable of more than 250,000 different expressions and that the face is responsible for most nonverbal messages" (Ibid, 1982). With all of those thousands of illustrative expressions, the possibility for misinterpretation is great. For a leader to become capable of analyzing facial expressions, he or she must realize that it is a personal discipline that must have continual, premeditated practice.

The following list of five items provides a foundation for reading and distinguishing nonverbal behavior.

1. Personal appearance: People's clothing and grooming present insight into their demeanor and their message. As with all nonverbal cues, personal appearances are situational and should be evaluated by their appropriateness in a particular setting.

Administrative Tip

Listening takes practice and effort. One exercise that highlights listening: See how many times in a conversation with a subordinate one can say "So what you are saying is…" By practicing this method of paraphrasing and repeating the message you heard, a coach or program administrator can strengthen his or her listening effectiveness. This constructive listening tactic also reassures the subordinates that they are being listened to and their transmission is important.

Administrative Tip

Communication is a two-way process. A coach or program administrator should continually observe his or her own nonverbal messages. Throughout the day, periodically stop and dissect nonverbal behavior. Introspectively examine personal appearance, personal spacing, posture, gestures, and timing. From the observations, determine if the nonverbal behaviors are appropriate for the situation and communication that is being attempted.

2. Personal space: An important signal of nonverbal communication is the maintenance of space between speaker and listener. For instance, the distance can connote comfort and confidence or uneasiness and skepticism (e.g., an intimate distance of 1-2 feet, a personal distance of 2-5 feet, a social distance of 5-10 feet, or a public distance of 10 or more feet).

3. Posture: Posture is another profound nonverbal message. For example, if a speaker's posture is brittle and restrictive, it could be concluded that the speaker is uncomfortable. Conversely, if a subordinate's physique is slumped and totally relaxed, boredom or apathy could be transmitted.

4. Appendages: The movement (or lack of movement) in body components such as arms, hands, feet, and legs can broadcast formidable signals. For example, a stationary person with arms folded across the chest could be conveying defensiveness.

5. Timing: The timing of a person's entrance into an interactive setting can disclose consequential nonverbal messages. If one is inexcusably tardy, a message of indifference and animosity could be conveyed, while punctuality could communicate interest and courtesy.

The list of nonverbal cues is endless. The assessment of those elements should be based on the circumstances and the individuals involved. Transforming a coach or program administrator into a person who can benefit from careful attention to both verbal and nonverbal cues is often difficult. It takes a diligent and calculated concentration. However, the payoff for this focused effort is immeasurable. This active technique cultivates staff and athlete retention, as well as enabling a coach or administrator to digest all information confidently, which is essential to effective leadership.

Situational Leadership

Because of the dynamic nature of our profession, coaches and program administrators must consciously avoid having a stagnant leadership style. The concept of one style and approach for all circumstances is outdated and will lead to ineffectual group leadership. Coaches and program administrators need to be situational evaluators of internal and external environments as well as of people. In other words, coaches and administrators need to assess situations and choose appropriate leadership responses. That is the underlying foundation of situational leadership.

Situational leaders are uniquely flexible in their observation of their surroundings. They look at every person, event, and environment as a distinct, exclusive challenge and understand that the challenges require individual responses instead of formatted reactions. In the simplest terms, for a coach or program administrator to become a situational leader, he or she needs to actively assess his or her surroundings and choose appropriate, definitive responses to maximize the program's potential.

Factors of Situational Leadership

There are some major components to becoming an effective situational leader.

1. Never forget that the coach or program administrator is the leader and decision maker for the team and program. This is easier said than done. Athletics involves emotions that might not be associated with or as intense as business management and leadership. Emotions can cloud decision making and, more importantly, behavior. In most of our administrative circumstances, we usually can control our emotions, which, in turn, can make situational leadership easier. In actual competitive situations, however, emotions can run high, and this makes recognition of the appropriate leadership tactic more difficult. To alleviate emotional debilitation, try to consciously recognize emotional states and use internal speech to reiterate one's leadership role. This will help one assess the situation and choose the right leadership approach.

2. Be true to oneself. Through our backgrounds, we all have developed personality traits and leadership styles (Appendix 4A delineates dominant styles). We must recognize these traits and become consciously aware of them in leadership situations. There are numerous leadership theories and test instruments that can objectively examine one's personality and leadership base. Confirm the findings by asking friends, family, and even athletes and staff if the assumptions and conclusions about one's personality are correct. Once a confirmed dominant style is identified, lock that information away. It will be the leadership base from which one will work.

3. Be true to the athletes and staff. Tell them up front what type of leadership base one has and how one will handle certain situations. The smaller the number of surprises, the less the apprehension and the greater the focus on message and task. For example, communicate to the staff and athletes that there will be a democratic and participative approach (see Appendix 4A) to setting individual and team goals. Conversely, tell them that in a competitive situation, the adoption of a more autocratic and authoritarian approach will be taken. Also, communicate to the staff and athletes that each situation that arises will be evaluated individually and an appropriate leadership approach chosen accordingly.

4. No matter what the situation or what decision must be made, every leadership action taken must be positive and in line with the program's pre-established goals and mission (Chapter 1). In the 1999 publication, *The Leadership Challenge*, Kouzes and Posner discuss tactics and approaches to leadership. In every instance, the underlying theme was optimism and positive actions. For example, one of their major leadership approaches deals with attracting people to a common purpose.

The common purpose is accomplished through a positive step-by-step process:

    a. Develop a shared sense of identity.

    b. Discover a common purpose.

    c. Give life to a vision.

    d. Demonstrate personal conviction.

    e. Commit to the challenge.

5. As previously reasoned: Become a good listener. Not only should one listen to people, but one should also listen to the environment in which the program operates.

6. Be equipped to handle a crisis or difficult situation. Whether on the court or off the field, a coach sometimes needs to lead quickly in take-charge situations.

When a take-charge situation occurs, take these steps immediately:

    1. Establish the objectives.

    2. Act boldly.

    3. Be decisive.

    4. Dominate the situation.

    5. Lead by example. (Cohen, 1990)

7. Maintain a positive concept of oneself by having self-confidence and truly believing that one can succeed. Self-confidence emanates from a person and is immediately recognized by a group. This, in turn, will have the group believing in one's abilities. Use the group's positive concept as an influencer in many situations. The higher the level of one's positive concept, the more accepting of the leadership a group will be. Unfortunately, the opposite is also true.

8. Learn more about leadership. There are countless textbooks, case studies, and self help books that cover the subject. After developing a knowledge base of leadership models (Appendices 4A, 4B, 4C), look inside our particular profession to find successful coaches and leaders. Ask questions. Just remember, one must be true to his or her own personality. What might be a successful approach for one person might not work for another in a particular situation.

Summary

Leadership is a perpetually transforming and increasingly essential topic for business managers. These leadership concepts relate clearly to our profession of coaching and program administration. Not only do we as coaches and program administrators need a foundation of theoretical knowledge, we also need to be competent in applying these philosophies in the daily operations of our programs. Concepts such as total quality management, effectual listening, and situational leadership are significant components of everyday operations and should be applied consistently as well as consciously.

APPENDIX 4A: Foundational Leadership Theories

Trait Theory

Trait theory is a leadership model constructed on "observed characteristics of a large number of successful and unsuccessful leaders. The resulting list of pertinent traits is then compared to potential leaders to predict their success or failure" (Hellriegel and Slocum, 1986). This simple method formed the first basis for predicting a leader's effectiveness. In other words, the theory's premise relies on similarity from one person to another. If one person is a successful leader with certain traits, another person with the same traits will also be successful. Even with the theory's subjective nature and obvious drawbacks, it appeals to an intrinsic component of human nature: to investigate a situation or person from the simplest and most straightforward criteria.

The theory examines both one's physical traits and one's personal disposition (psyche). Physical traits are the easiest to determine because of their manifested appearance. Historically, our ancestors were often barbaric leaders with tremendous physical strength, size, and agility. As our civilization evolved, the advancements in technology accentuated intellect over anatomical distinctions. From the progression, the trait theory attempts to assemble mannerisms, habits, and idiosyncratic distinctions into systematic categories. Most empirical studies of the trait theory suggest that there are four traits that are commonly shared by most (but not all) successful leaders. These traits:

Intelligence—Leaders tend to have somewhat higher intellectual abilities than their followers.

Maturity and Breadth—Leaders tend to be emotionally mature and have a broad range of interests.

Inner Motivation and Achievement Driven—Leaders want to accomplish objectives; when they achieve one goal, they seek out another. They do not depend on others for their inner motivation to achieve.

People Centered—Leaders are able to work effectively with other people in a variety of situations. They respect others and realize that to accomplish tasks, they must be considerate of others (Ibid, 1986).

It should be emphasized that the trait approach is an incomplete leadership theory. Its most serious drawback is its omission of environmental factors, societal values and norms, and other contextual background elements.

Authoritarian/Democratic/Laissez Faire Theory

The most widely known of all leadership theories is based on the behavioral distinctions between authoritarian, democratic, and laissez faire styles. The following is a breakdown of these three universally standardized styles (also known as *autocratic*, *participative*, and *abdicative*).

Authoritarian/Autocratic

The authoritarian method of leadership is the unbending employment of legitimate power inherent in the position of management (or in our case, coach or program administrator). The flow of decisions is from a top-down hierarchal system in which all administrative decrees and decisions by a leader are absolute and unyielding. The style utilizes straightforward accountability expectations that are clear, logical, and comprehensible. The most common settings for the application of authoritarian leadership are military and medical settings that rely on orders given and carried out.

> The primary problem with the authoritarian/autocratic leadership approach is that workers are made aware of what to do but not why. This often leads to 1) low employee morale and 2) workers following leader's directions to the letter, even if those directions are wrong. . . thus, the authoritarian style, while satisfying to the leader's needs, may cause employees (staff and athletes) to avoid responsibility, initiative, and innovation. (Gray and Stark, 1988)

Conversely, if a leader is respected and has a long track record of success and if the situation is receptive to this technique, the advantages range from timely accomplishment of tasks to the focus of a single vision.

Democratic/Participative

The democratic leadership approach to decision making is diametrically opposite from the authoritarian style. "Democratic/participative leaders let subordinates actively participate in operational decision making. . . which has shown a consistent positive relationship to participant satisfaction and accomplishment" (Stearns and Aldag, 1987). This style accomplishes production and goal achievement through group consensus and acceptance. The most distinguished utilization of the democratic style in our society and culture is through our structured governmental political system.

As with all leadership methodologies, the environment in which a leader is operating will influence the style of leadership. Our society is founded and governed on the philosophical principles of democracy. From this perspective, one could assume that this doctrine is suitable for all facets of our lives. This assumption is invalid. For example, emergencies in our society would have disastrous consequences if the professional involved (whether it be a doctor, firefighter, or police officer) utilized the democratic leadership style. The best example of this would be in the case of an E.R. medical emergency. By the time the doctor finishes polling all for their opinion, the patient might have already died. This example can be used via analogy for coaching. By the time the coach gets through polling staff and players for their input, the game could already be over and lost.

If the situation warrants the use of the democratic method, the benefits are numerous. Some benefits:

- soliciting more input and information from a wider variety of individuals gives a decision maker a different perspective.
- an elevated sense of group morale.
- staff and players having a vested interest in the decisions and outcomes.
- a rejuvenated organizational focus on goals.

Laissez Faire/Abdicated

The final leadership style of laissez faire/abdicated is best described as a profile of leadership that is "easygoing and makes little attempt to direct and organize a group. . . laissez faire leaders are usually ineffectual in organizational situations because the group lacks directives and tackles problems in a haphazard way" (Robertson, 1987). From a coaching or program administration perspective, this leadership philosophy is very irrational, incoherent, and should rarely be exercised. This technique has organizational personnel (staff and players) setting goals and individualizing work ethics and operational policies. With no direction, staff members and players will set their own agendas, in their own timeframes, and by their own guidelines. The only conceivable circumstance in which this approach could be utilized would be in a sedate, leisurely environment where achieving goals within a given timeframe is not a priority.

McGregor's Theory X and Theory Y

Another widely recognized leadership theory is McGregor's Theory X and Theory Y. Douglas McGregor, a student of Abraham Maslow (Theory of Hierarchical Needs), probed leadership from two contradictory perspectives. These perspectives examined a manager's opinions, conclusions, and feelings toward his or her subordinates.

His two-pronged theory is as follows (extrapolated from Griffin and Moorehead, 1986):

Theory X argues:

1. People do not like work and try to avoid it.
2. People do not like work, so managers have to control, direct, coerce, and threaten employees to get them to work toward organizational goals.
3. People prefer to be directed, to avoid responsibility, to want security; they have little ambition.
4. Employees are only motivated by psychological and primary safety needs.

Theory Y argues:

1. People do not dislike work; work is a part of their lives.
2. People are internally motivated to reach objectives to which they are committed.

3. People are committed to goals to the degree that they receive personal rewards when they reach their objectives.
4. People will both seek and accept responsibility under favorable conditions.
5. People have the capacity for innovation in solving problem situations.
6. People are bright, but under most circumstances and organizational conditions, their potential is underutilized.

Theories X and Y voice the extremes on the spectrum of leadership thought. The astringent, pessimistic X speculations correlate with the authoritarian style, while the Y theory aligns itself with the employee-centered, democratic approach.

In his 1960 text, *The Human Side of the Enterprise*, McGregor accentuates the idea that a leader's attitude and disposition toward the employees (staff and players) is the determining factor for their happiness and productivity. If a leader's attitude toward subordinates is that all subordinates are lethargic, lackadaisical, unmotivated, and untrustworthy, the organization's employees will impulsively react precisely to these predetermined notions and expectations. In other words, the leader's or coach's attitude and style establish the basis for the subordinate's self-fulfilling prophecy. With this in mind, McGregor focuses a preponderance of his text on the practical application of Theory Y.

McGregor stresses that the best way to integrate Theory Y thinking into the organization is through "the creation of conditions such that the members of the organization, group, or team can achieve their own goals best by directing their efforts toward the success of the organization" (McGregor, 1960). If the coach or program administrator can prioritize the needs of individuals within the parameters of team goals, Theory Y will be a reality. The benefits of a Theory Y environment include an inspired, goal-oriented team that stresses maximizing of talent and innovation in every player and staff member. The concept is simple, but it has tremendous potential. It should be noted that

> the acceptance of Theory Y does not imply abdication, soft management, or permissiveness. . . such notions stem from the acceptance of authority as the single means of managerial control. Theory Y assumes that people will exercise self-direction and self-control in the achievement of organizational objectives to the degree that they are committed to those objectives. The theory does not deny the appropriateness of authority, but does deny that authority is appropriate for all circumstances. (McGregor, 1960)

Blake and Mouton's Managerial Grid

The managerial grid is a matrix that interprets leadership within two central leadership dimensions. The leadership matrix is structured by a dimension of concern for people and a dimension of concern for production. Each of these directional approaches is divided into nine zones, one

Figure 1 Blake and Mouton's Managerial Grid (Blake and Mouton, 1978)

```
                              High People

          9  1,9 Country Club Management              9,9 Team Management
          8
          7
   Low    6
Production 5            5,5 Middle of the Road Management        High
          4                                                   Production
          3
          2
          1  1,1 Impoverished Management        9,1 Authoritarian Obedience
             1      2     3     4     5     6     7     8     9

                              Low People
```

being the lowest and nine being the highest. Thus the grid yields an 81-point graph surface that is used to illustrate and analyze managerial behavior by the simple philosophy of people oriented, production oriented, or a combination of both.

> To describe all of the 81 points on the grid would miss the purpose of the matrix; researchers' abilities to distinguish behavior of leaders in work situations are far from that precisely developed. Instead, Blake and Mouton prefer to describe five extreme positions on the grid. (Parce and Robinson, 1989)

1. 9,1 Leader, **Authoritarian Obedience-of-Task Leader** is a task-focused manager who highlights all factors of productivity but distances him- or herself from all interpersonal interactions. This type of leader perceives camaraderie with subordinates as counterproductive.

2. 1,9 Leader, **Country Club or Good Neighbor Leader** has little or no interest for end results, productivity, or decision making. He or she is considered a people-centered administrator.

3. 5,5 Leader, **Middle-of-the-Road Leader** embraces compromise between people and productivity. This approach is consistent and reserved, but lacks innovation and upward motivation.

4. 1,1 Leader, **Impoverished Leader** is, by all definitions, never actually a leader. This manager is nonresponsive and apathetic toward people and results.

5. 9,9 Leader, **Team Manager/Leader** is the consummate professional tenaciously dedicated to the organization and sympathetic and empathetic toward employee concerns.

Figure 2: House's Path-Glory Leadership (House, 1974)

Style: **Directive Leadership**
Behavior:
- Define group's task goals.
- Assign specific task responsibilities.
- Closely supervise employees.
- Use formal authority to manage employees.

Situation:
- The group's tasks are unstructured.
- Employees expect guidance.

Style: **Supportive Leadership**
Behavior:
- Be friendly and appropriate.
- Show personal interest in employees.
- Strive for harmony.
- Use rewards to gain support.

Situation:
- The group's tasks lack intrinsic motivation.
- Employees expect supportive behavior.

Style: **Participative Leadership**
Behavior:
- Allow employee to make decisions.
- Encourage teamwork.
- Use informal power bases.
- Share performance responsibilities.

Situation:
- Tasks are complex and require teamwork.
- Employees have job skills.
- Employees desire some level of control.

Style: **Achievement Leadership**
Behavior:
- Encourage employees to set high performance standards.
- Allow them to be on their own.
- Manage employees by results.

Situation:
- Employees desire self-control.
- Employees are achievement oriented.
- Employees have needed skills.

The Path-Glory Theory of Leadership is similar to previous leadership models in defining certain leadership approaches. House's model differs in that it identifies situations in which one should apply a certain leadership style. The four leadership styles:

1. **Directive**—The leader directs and there is no subordinate participation in decision-making.
2. **Supportive**—The leader is friendly and is interested in subordinates as people.
3. **Participative**—The leader asks for, receives, and uses suggestions from subordinates to make decisions.
4. **Achievement Oriented**—The leader sets challenges and goals for subordinates and shows confidence that they can achieve those goals. (Donnelly, Gibson, and Ivencevich, 1987)

Hersey and Blanchard's Leadership Theory

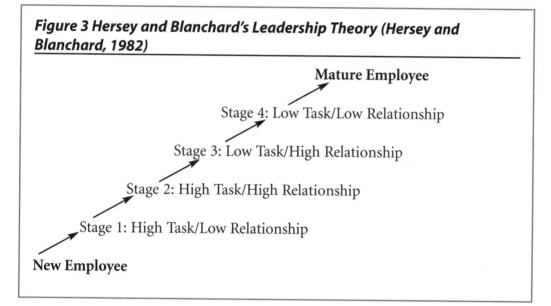

Figure 3 Hersey and Blanchard's Leadership Theory (Hersey and Blanchard, 1982)

Mature Employee

Stage 4: Low Task/Low Relationship

Stage 3: Low Task/High Relationship

Stage 2: High Task/High Relationship

Stage 1: High Task/Low Relationship

New Employee

The Hersey and Blanchard Leadership Model is founded on the concept that the maturity (time in a program) of the subordinate (whether staff or athlete) will dictate the level of people or task leadership behavior. Within each of the four stages of a subordinate's program maturity, a different combination of task and people relationship behavior should be applied.

Stage 1: High Task/Low Relationship—In this stage, the new subordinate (player or coach) should be initiated into the program's operations by punctuating a high task environment with minimal people- or relationship-oriented leadership. As the coach, one should act in the directive mode employing a one-way communication system that teaches the new subordinate job responsibilities and tasks to be performed. Close supervision and straightforward instructions will be utilized, which in turn, will eliminate any apprehension from undefined expectations.

Stage 2: High Task/High Relationship—Following the indoctrination of task responsibilities in stage one, stage two emphasizes high task and high relationship. Even though the subordinates are still being directly supervised, the high relationship aspect fosters familiarity, trust, and communication between a coach and his or her player or staff member.

Stage 3: Low Task/High Relationship—In this maturity period, the subordinate has become proficient at his or her position and needs little or no direct task supervision. High relationship-oriented leadership is still employed for the cultivation and fortification of a subordinate's continued performance. This stage manifests an open communication system that will bring innovation and creativity from the subordinate.

Stage 4: Low Task/Low Relationship—The final stage in the model represents the completion of the subordinate's organizational maturity. He or she has mastered assignments and tasks and is capable of exerting self-discipline and motivation. The coach should have absolute confidence in delegating and empowering any previously learned skill. Little or no emotional support is needed.

The key to utilizing the model in a practical application is to become an insightful, receptive coach. One needs to comprehend the subordinate's responsibilities as well as his or her timeframe for transition through the stages. Some subordinates will advance through stages more quickly than others.

APPENDIX 4B: Contemporary Theories of Leadership

Theory 1

In his 1980 text, *The Management Option*, David L. Sudhalter canvasses the idea of leadership from a linear, concrete vantage point. He expounds on 10 distinct qualities that all good leaders are seen to have:

1. To be able to inspire and motivate others.
2. To be able to delegate authority at the right times, to the right people, under the right conditions.
3. To be at least able to see just around the corner, by developing and utilizing the powers of perception.
4. To be able to plan and organize activities of the operation.
5. To have the ability to maintain harmony and equilibrium in an organization.
6. To be able to assume the responsibility for the organization, not only when things go well, but also when they go badly.
7. To be a competent spokesman for the organization's subordinates as well as the entire organization.
8. To be able to negotiate effectively.
9. To be able to manage a crisis calmly.
10. To be able to set reasonable goals that can be accomplished.

Theory 2

From a more philosophical viewpoint, Abram Collier, in his 1992 article, "Business Leadership and a Creative Society," states that the greatest function of leadership is that the leader expresses, for his or her group, the ideals toward which they all, consciously or unconsciously, strive. What in truth do I seek? What objectives do I have that my employees can share? On this view, the first task of business leadership is to create an environment that can flourish not only for a single, creative genius, but more importantly, for the collective capacities of all the people in the organization.

Theory 3

John Adams, in *Transformational Leadership: From Vision to Results*, scrutinizes the concept of leadership from a strategic action approach. His philosophical position is to suppress our normal tendencies, as leaders, of wanting to. . .

1. Solve problems quickly.
2. Maintain predictability, consistency, and status quo.
3. Reflect on the past, reacting to events after they happen to correct deviations.
4. Think in predominately rational analytical modes.
5. Break situations down into their smallest parts as the means to understanding.

6. Be controlled by external circumstances.

Adams also declares that leadership should be a strategic operation based on the following summarized premises.

Premise One: Leadership is a state of consciousness rather than a personal trait or a set of skills. The leadership state of consciousness sways individuals to

- become self aware.
- live with and value ambiguity.
- create and work with alternative choices, structures, and systems.
- encourage differences and seek the gifts each person has to offer.
- experience the absence of chances as potentially disruptive to high performance.
- reward risks taken in service of vision.
- develop flexible temporary structures.

Premise Two: A primary role of a leader is to activate, establish, and nurture a focus on vision, purpose, and outcomes. Establishing and holding a vision of desired outcomes greatly increases the possibility of realizing them.

Premise Three: It is cost effective to empower the workforce. Once a vision is shared, the leader needs to remove constraints to inspire performance. A leader must strategically provide conditions that. . .

- create a clear purpose and direction.
- encourage opportunities for innovation.
- seek an individual's potential and gently demand excellence.
- establish and gain commitment to high but attainable standards.
- create challenging, meaningful assignments.
- acknowledge and celebrate success.
- set examples of excellence.
- hold to agreements.
- capitalize on individual differences.
- allow a wide latitude of self-expression.

Premise Four: A systems perspective is necessary to avoid emphasis on alleviating symptoms. Each functional part of the organization has its own parochial perspective or interpretation of what should be done. What is needed is the coordination of all functions through a systems perspective and shared vision of the whole organization.

Premise Five: Attention to needed support systems is essential to achieving the vision. On the structural level, it is essential that the leader be aware of how adequately various support mechanisms are facilitating desired outcomes. It is not at all unusual to find that a system defeats itself because procedures to get an essential task accomplished are not in place. One of the most frequent reasons why strategic planning does not work is that, as time passes, the accountability for implementing key actions becomes ambiguous, and everyone waits for someone else to initiate them.

Theory 4

Weston H. Agor expounds on a totally different angle of leadership: intuition. In *Intuition in Organizations*, he stresses that the emphasis, rightly due to strategic, linear, and philosophical positions (as well as other theories) of leadership, should be strongly augmented by an intuitive thought. He states that intuition is becoming more critical in today's organizational context for several reasons:

- There is a high level of uncertainty.
- There tends to be few precedents.
- Reliable facts are limited or unavailable.
- Time is limited and there is an ever-increasing pressure to be right.
- There are several plausible options to choose from, all of which can be supported by factual arguments.

He concludes with the statement that if one hopes to be better prepared for tomorrow, then it only seems logical to pay some attention to the development of intuitive leadership and decision-making skills today.

Theory 5

Jay Conger, in the 1989 publication, *The Charismatic Leader*, emphasizes the leadership element of charisma as the most important component of leadership. His four-stage charismatic model of leadership defines leadership as the process of moving an organization from an existing state to some future state as described in Figure 4.

Figure 4: Conger's Behavioral Dimension Model (Conger, 1989)

Stage 1

Detect Unexploited Opportunities and Deficiencies in the Present Situation
High Sensitivity to Constituents' Needs
Formulating an Idealized Strategic Vision

Stage 2

Communicating the Vision
Articulating the Status Quo as Unacceptable and the Vision as the Most Attractive Alternative
Articulate Motivation to Lead the Followers

Stage 3

Build Trust Through Success, Expertise, Personal Risk Taking, Self-Sacrifice, and Unconventional Behavior

Stage 4

Demonstrate the Means to Achieve the Vision Though Modeling, Empowerment, and Unconventional Tactics

---

Theory 6

Through books such as *Tough Minded Management* (1978), *Expectations and Possibilities* (1981), and *Tough Minded Leadership* (1989), Joe Batten has constructed a twelve-phase, cyclical leadership theory. Batten's cybernetic circle of leadership is a philosophical declaration that provides fundamental infrastructure for organizational leadership. The twelve-phase, cyclical doctrine is as follows:

1. Clarify purpose and direction
2. Ask, listen, and hear
3. Enable involvement and participation
4. Set clear expectations and goals
5. Provide consistent interaction
6. Affirm and optimize strengths
7. Establish measurements
8. Monitor performance
9. Provide developmental counsel
10. Establish accountability
11. Make tough-minded decisions
12. Expect excellence

Narrative Elaboration:

1. The concept of clarification of operational direction and purpose is to consolidate and focus the organization's personnel toward one collective, unified mission.
2. The leadership objective associated with the function of inquiring, listening, and hearing is the active utilization of the organization's human resource. Through a responsive, two-way communication system, businesses and athletic programs can access a wide variety of potential ideas and impressions from their personnel.
3. Successful leadership energetically solicits the involvement and participation of subordinates. This vantage furnishes pertinent information that, in turn, resolves operational problems and fulfills program goals.
4. Unequivocal, precise expectations give significant clarification to a subordinate.
5. Consistent interaction deals with the beneficial communication process (discussed in Appendix 4C) between leaders and subordinates. For a situation and a leader in that situation to be effective, the ongoing and reciprocal exchange of ideas, facts, and data must be transmitted in a logical, understandable fashion.
6. Competent, skillful leadership affirms and employs an organization's strengths.
7. The conclusions of measuring instruments (both qualitative and quantitative) provide subordinates with direction and benchmarks to measure performance.
8. Performance monitoring optimizes personnel motivation and measures operational success.

9. Career advice, professional consultations, and informal subordinate planning are directly related to a leader's interaction capabilities. Unpretentious and down-to-earth leaders will continuously consult employees (staff and athletes) on their progress toward personal and professional goals in a warm and caring manner.

10. Straightforward performance assignments will eradicate the possibility of program miscommunication as well as eliminate apprehension from unclear standards among staff and athletes.

11. Leaders need to make aggressive, accurate decisions. They need to solicit support from subordinates for these decisions whenever possible. Likewise, if the decision is unpopular, a leader must be willing to stand by his/her decision.

12. Anticipation of excellence displays confidence in staff/athletes and standardizes high quality in all actions.

Batten stresses that the cybernetic circle of leadership is a continuous process. For example, after a manager (coach or administrator) has concluded an endeavor, project, or athletic season, he or she will once again begin at step one by re-establishing the organization's mission and direction for the next operational endeavor.

Theory 7

Kouzes and Posner, in their 1999 publication, *The Leadership Challenge*, hypothesize that leadership is an indoctrinated, observed function that is attainable by anyone, in any capacity. They feel that if a committed, dedi-

---

Figure 5: Kouzes and Posner's 10 Behavioral Commitments of Leadership (Kouzes and Posner, 1997)

Challenge the Process

Search for Opportunities
Experiment and Take Risks

Inspire a Shared Vision

Envision the Future
Enlist Others and Enable Others to Act
Foster Collaboration
Strengthen Others

Model the Way

Set the Example
Plan Small Wins

Encourage the Heart

Recognize Individual Contributions
Celebrate Contributions

---

cated individual would emulate their 10 behavioral commitments, this person would become a proactive, successful leader. They have constructed their principles from research surveys of more than 500 contemporary, successful leaders. Success in this context is interpreted as being perceived credibility; meeting and surpassing performance expectations; and being future oriented, impartial and equitable, imaginative, and broadminded.

Narrative Elaboration:

1. Search for opportunities: This leadership obligation proactively institutes change. It appraises plausible opportunities and manipulates each opportunity for organizational goal achievement.

2. Experiment and take risks: This behavioral commitment embraces organizational communication channels (internal and external) to envision opportunities; it cultivates and encourages leaders to go beyond personal restraints; it disciplines leaders to learn from each other's mistakes.

3. Envision the future: This leadership perspective observes the future from what is achievable from past tendencies and patterns.

4. Enlist others: This behavioral responsibility embraces open communication channels and accentuates the conviction that no thought or idea is right or wrong, better or worse; it enlists subordinates through formal one-on-one sessions and collective group brainstorming.

5. Foster collaboration: This leadership tactic works through the development of a participative mission and builds a trust foundation for organizational continuation.

6. Strengthen others: Leaders who nurture a subordinate's strengths will not only provide new opportunities for the group and organization but will also earn the long-term commitment of the subordinates.

7. Set the example: Leaders lead by example and should participate in all operational activities (in some capacity). This hands-on demeanor develops teamwork and camaraderie that, in turn, increase productivity.

8. Plan small wins: Leaders should integrate a plan of small program wins. This step-by-step game plan consolidates positive short-term goals into projected organizational missions.

9. Recognize individual contributions: Effective leaders enable others to perform by establishing high but achievable expectations. Performance standards as motivational tools should be associated with tangible rewards (whenever possible). Leaders who provide accolades as performance incentives should actively pursue individuals who are purposeful, tenacious, and exceed performance requirements.

10. Celebrate accomplishment: Leadership behavioral commitments should publicly acknowledge outstanding and timely task achievements.

Theory 8

In his original text, *Principles of Technical Management,* and in his later 1990 publication, *The Art of the Leader,* Cohen provides five straightforward keys to effective leadership problem solving:

1. Always ask the question: Why?
2. Break complicated problems into less complicated components
3. Increase the number of alternatives under consideration.
4. Don't try to keep all problem-solving facts in one's head when making decisions.
5. Consider the consequences of each alternative decision.

Narrative Elaboration:

1. Ask "Why?": This crucial question develops a leader's alternatives by confronting every declaration and explanation. A leader who blindly endorses customary answers without interrogation is limiting his or her talents and managerial options.

2. Break down complicated problems into less complicated components: The complexity of some leadership obstacles can overwhelm a leader and deter actions. The logical dissection of problems into small segments will allow a more sequential, concentrated effort on smaller, simpler components rather than the catch-all approach of aggregate problem solving.

3. Increase the number of alternatives: Increasing alternatives provides leaders with more latitude on deciding which alternative is the best.

4. Record all factual information: No one individual is flawless and can recollect all minute parts of a situation. The capable application of notes and other recording instruments assures that a leader will not disregard or omit any element in the problem-solving process.

5. Evaluate the consequences: Simply express each alternative under consideration by its ramifications for the organization/program. These results will need to be analyzed as to their probability and operational repercussions.

Appendix 4C: The Communication Process for Leaders

In their 1988 publication, *Business Communication: Strategies and Solutions*, Baird and Stull elucidate a step-by-step analysis of the communication process for leaders. The communication process steps:

1. Getting an idea
2. Determining a goal
3. Choosing a medium
4. Encoding a message
5. Decoding a message
6. Receiving feedback

Getting an Idea: The beginning of any two-way communication is through the formation of an idea. The indicator (sender) of a communication must first experience, either internally or externally, an environmental stimulation that prompts and activates the desire to communicate. Internal features are from associations, recognition, and contemplation. External stimuli encompass the aggregate entirety of all situational components. In other words, the communication process begins with perceptions, thoughts, outside information, and meanings.

Determining a Goal: The fundamental motivation for communication is the intelligible conveying of an idea. This routine is typically accomplished within a split second. For example, in a majority of interpersonal communications, the thought process of idea generation and the broadcasting of the information are virtually concurrent. Conversely, in more formal com-

---

Figure 6: Internal and External Organizational Communication Mediums (Murphy and Heildebrant, 1988)

Internal

Written	**Oral**
Memos	Staff Meetings
Reports	Face-to-Face Interactions
Bulletins	Speeches
Job Descriptions	Audio Tapes
Notes	Telephone Conferences
Posters	
Manuals	

External

Written	**Oral**
Letters	Speeches
Proposals	Video Conferences
Telegrams	Interviews
Reports	Telephone/Teleconferences
Brochures	Face-to-Face Interactions
Cable/Mail Grams/E-Mails	

munication, intuitions, intentions, and purposes are more intensely scrutinized for the avoidance of misinterpretations and inadequacies. Whether the initiator intentionally considers the communication objective or instantaneously communicates an idea or feeling, goals are being established and fulfilled.

Choosing a Medium: How should the message be transmitted? Media (or communication instruments) can comprise verbal/oral channels, written/graphic symbols, or nonverbal unwritten/gestures and body movements. From a program vantage, the determination of the type of medium to be used is contingent on whether the message receiver is inside or outside the organization.

The principal influences on the development of a particular type of medium:
1. Formality desired.
2. Relationship established.
3. Intimacy between sender and receiver.
4. Response expected.
5. Gravity of communication.
6. Sender's dexterity and expertise with different types of media.
7. Receiver's comprehension and receptiveness of medium.
8. Time restrictions.
9. Cost and resource expenditures.

Encoding a Message: After the selection of the medium to impart the message, the sender must determine the ideal diction, expression, and wording to communication the idea. The term *encoding* refers to the selection of the appropriate symbols and vocabulary. The difficulties and pitfalls in encoding messages have to do with the elimination of possible misinterpretations. Misunderstandings can arise from disparate meanings of words and symbols, a lack of common frames of reference, individual backgrounds and education, etc.

Decoding a Message: Whether the message is orally stated, transcribed, or conveyed through body gestures and other nonverbal communication, the decoding procedure is dependent upon the person's
1. Understanding of the content.
2. Experience with similar messages, including subject matter and the words used to explain it.
3. The receiver's ability to deal with any communication barriers and breakdowns. (Baird, 1977)

The concept of communication barriers and breakdowns is discussed further in the appendix section of the chapter.

Feedback: Feedback is characterized as a response to a communication. The feedback response can be reactive, impulsive, and instinctive or it can be cerebral and contemplative. The receiver's interpretation of the message will determine his/her response. If the communication is precise and interpreted correctly, the response is likely to be anticipated and coherent. If the communication is misinterpreted, the feedback response is usually incongruent and unexpected. After this stage, the sender becomes the receiver.

The significance of feedback in any organization cannot be overstated. With the lack of adequate feedback, managers can only hope that a communication has been received and comprehended. There tends to be a trend in most organizations to devalue feedback, which, in turn, makes most subordinates apprehensive about conveying feedback.

There are two distinct advantages of feedback, three arguable disadvantages, and eight methods for improving organizational communication feedback. The advantages:

1. Feedback increases the accuracy of employee understanding and performance. Misunderstandings (which can be expensive) are minimized.
2. Feedback increases employee job satisfaction. Feedback encourages ideas and opinions while tending to make employees feel closer to the operation.

The arguable disadvantages:

1. Feedback can cause recipients to feel psychologically under attack. People can become defensive if feedback seems negative and overwhelming.
2. Feedback is time consuming.
3. Feedback is difficult to elicit. People have strong tendencies to avoid saying that they don't understand. They feel that others will perceive them adversely.

To improve the communication process and feedback, Hamilton and Parker suggest the following:

1. Tell people openly that feedback is wanted.
2. Identify areas where feedback is needed.
3. Set aside time for regular feedback sessions.
4. Use silence to encourage feedback.
5. Be cognizant of and watch for nonverbal responses.
6. Ask pertinent questions.
7. Use statements that encourage feedback.
8. Reward feedback. (Hamilton and Parker, 1987)

Barriers and breakdowns: Barriers and breakdowns in the communication process are principally described by scholars as transmission noises. Noise can be from peripheral, external sources or from cognitive, internal sources. External sources can be audible noises such as traffic sounds, poor enunciation, slurred speech, and other background clutter that obscure the communication. Other external factors that can cause a breakdown in the communication process can include room temperature, lighting, odors, and other superficial factors that physically affect a person's senses. Internal noises can be from preoccupation, emotional and mental distress, ignorance on the subject discussed, daydreaming, etc.

Figure 2 is a pictorial summary of the communication process.

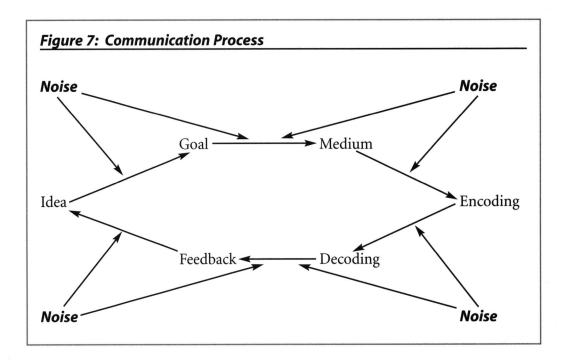

Figure 7: Communication Process

Chapter 5 ....
Control

Introduction

This chapter is the last of the five chapters in the section on management concepts. It examines the depth and application of the managerial function of control and the elements in the control process.

In theory, and if done correctly, the first four concepts of management (planning, organizing, human resource management, and leadership) minimize and sometimes preempt the concept of control. However, in the real world, the function of managerial and athletic program control is essential for facilitating operations and accomplishing goals.

Control Defined

The word *control* has a unique meaning to each of us. For the most part, the business world has defined the functional duty of control as a standardized, simple, and step-by-step process (see subsection entitled The Control Process). The applicable definition is "as a management process, controlling is the function of ensuring that the organization's objectives and goals are

Administrative Tip

Control is the ultimate step in the management process and leads right back into the first step, planning. In other words, management is a circular progression with no beginning or end.

being attained" (Mescon, 1981). From this definition, the importance of the planning process in giving an organization and athletic program focus is accentuated. Without delineated goals there would be nothing to control. This leads to the question, "Why practice managerial controls"?

Why Practice Managerial Controls?

Managerial controls

> alert managers [in our case, coaches and program administrators] to potentially critical problems. . . problems occur when organizational goals are not being met. Controls are designed to give managers [coaches and program administrators] information regarding the following:
>
> 1. Prevent crises—it is easy for small, readily solved problems to turn into crises.
> 2. Standardize outputs—improve quality and quantity through the use of good controls.
> 3. Appraise employee's performances—provide objective information about employee performances and outcomes.
> 4. Update plans—the best plans need to be updated as changes occur.
> 5. Protect an organization's assets—controls protect a program's assets from ineffectual waste. (Rue and Byars, 1992)

These five major reasons to practice managerial controls can be related to coaching and athletic program administration.

Through proactive planning and control, all coaches should try to avoid crisis management. Because our end product is often our program's and athletes' performances, not some type of developmental plan or the quality control of an athlete's training, poor planning and a lack of control could lead not only to the athlete failing but also to the failure of the whole program. The possible crisis situations in an athletic program are unlimited. However, with strong control systems in place, the program can minimize the possibility of a small problem turning into a major crisis.

Standardizing outputs emphasizes quality control and maximization of resources. As discussed in previous chapters, quality should be a primary goal in all aspects of the athletic program. If the control system and philosophy stress standardized quality, then the program will consistently produce quality outputs and performances.

In appraising employees, control revolves around maximizing an athlete's or staff member's skills and capabilities. By their very nature, performance evaluations are direct tools that keep the program's personnel focused, not only on their personal goals but also on the program's goals. The maintenance on this type of control system has a direct effect on productivity and performance.

A business or program plan must foremost be considered a flexible document that can be adapted and revised. In most cases, the only way to

Administrative Tip

A coach or program administrator should view control as a continuum. At one end of the continuum is the lack of control and at the other end is micromanagement. While the damages of a lack of control are clear, micromanagement is just as perilous. A good control system and personal philosophy should balance these two diametrically opposite positions.

determine if an element of the program plan needs adjusting is to examine that element over time. Through good monitoring and controls, one can determine what goals and objectives are still relevant and which targeted plans need to be adjusted (expanded, augmented, minimized, eliminated).

Finally, all programs (no matter how large) have limited resources. Control systems can quickly determine which functions are effectively using program resources (time, money, manpower) and which are not. For example, the program might be utilizing a certain training technique to develop a particular skill or strength. Without proper controls and monitoring, how could one know if this technique is a productive training method or if the program could use its time/resources/efforts more effectively elsewhere?

Types of Controls

In his text, *Management,* Holt defines "three types of controls that lead to different decisions. They are steering controls, yes/no controls, and post action controls" (1990). The three concepts are broken down as follows:

1. Steering controls are used to adjust behavior while the program's operations are in progress. This control method keeps the program on track and avoids tangents. A small change early in a process can avoid a large change and restructuring later.
2. Yes/No controls are essentially go/no-go decisions at selected checkpoints in the program's operations. The key to this type of control process is discovering the points at which to make a go/no-go decision. Typically, these are called the "points of no return" or critical decision junctions. For example, the hardest type of yes/no decisions in our profession of coaching relates to the retention or dismissal of athletes. In this scenario, whether one personally determines the "cutdown" date or the program's governing body (NCAA, MLB, High School Association, etc.) does, the coach or program administrator has a program decision. . . does the program go with an athlete or is he or she released? Once again, the control decision is based on the program's goals and mission.
3. Post-action controls are the comparison of actual with projected results after a specific time period has elapsed. This a major premise behind the control process.

The Control Process

Before an elaboration of each step is given, it must be emphasized that the control process is not a separate, stand-alone element of the management concept but an integrated feature of management. Furthermore, while the process of control is essentially sequential, the actual variety of applications of the control process inside the program is unlimited. For the process to be effective, it must be an ongoing activity rather than an intermittent and occasional event.

Administrative Tip

As with most managerial functions, enlist the whole program in the control process. This will give each staff member and athlete a motivated, vested interest in the execution of control as well as a lucid understanding of control procedures in the program.

Figure 1: The Control Process (Bedian, 1993)

Establish Performance Standards

↓

Determine Performance Measurements

↓

Measure Performance

↓

Compare With Standards Established

↓

Take Corrective Action (If Neccessary)

Establish Performance Standards

The first factor in the control process is establishing performance standards. "A standard is a target against which subsequent performance is to be compared. . . standards established for control purposes should be derived directly from the organization's goals" (Griffin, 1990). The planning aspect of the management process stresses that the program determine specific, tangible, and measurable goals. For example, from an academic standpoint in either high school or college, one of the program goals could be to achieve a team grade point average of 3.0 on a 4.0 scale. To accomplish this, the staff, athletes, and team could determine that the following elements are critical for the athletes and program to reach their academic projected goal:

1. Class attendance and participation.
2. Midterm, finals, and other tests.
3. Term papers and extra credit.

Now establish objective performance standards for each of these targeted performance ingredients. For example:

1. Each athlete must attend at least 90% of all classes and take an active role in all discussions.
2. Each athlete must achieve a score of 75% or higher on all planned exams.
3. All term papers must achieve a score of 80% or higher and all homework assignments must be completed in a timely manner.

Can establishing performance standards be utilized for individuals as well as teams? Absolutely. For example, in the sport of baseball, the coach and athlete can discuss a personal baseball goal of hitting .300 for a particular season. Both concur that the following performance elements are fundamental in fulfilling that goal:

1. Bat speed must increase.
2. More repetitions in practice.
3. Feedback and instruction on techniques.

Administrative Tip

When establishing performance standards, use historical data and standards as the starting point but do not finish there. Question what other similar and successful athletic programs have instituted as their performance standards. By merging the competition's standards with information on historical foundations, a coach or program administrator can develop specific controls that are rational as well as realistic.

Now jointly establish performance standards for each element. For instance:

1. Bat speed must increase by 20%. More intense weight lifting and strength conditioning are employed.
2. After each practice session, the athlete (along with the coaching staff) hits 50 to 100 extra balls.
3. After each game, the coach and the athlete evaluate the game film.

It should be noted that goals and performance standards have to be based in reality. One's mission as a program administrator and leader should be to establish goals and standards that are challenging and achievable rather than discouraging and unrealistic.

Determine Performance Measurements

The preceding examples arbitrarily determined which performance measurements were to be utilized to achieve goals. Megginson, Mosley, and Pietri have identified some important considerations in choosing which performance factors one should select in establishing standards to reach targeted goals.

These important considerations are found in the following questions:

1. How often should performance be measured?
2. What form will the measurement take?
3. Who will be involved in measuring performances?
4. Is it cost and time effective?
5. Is it capable of being explained? (Megginson, Mosley, and Pietri, 1983)

Obviously, the more important the individual or program goal, the more critical the above questions become. Additionally, as time goes by, the coach or program administrator will be more adept in determining the performance standards that correlate most directly with the program's goals and, hence, are more useful.

Measure Performance

There are two ways to measure performance: One is through quantitative valuation; The other is qualitative, subjective observation. Many business organizations adhere strictly to the philosophy of judging performance according to the "bottom line results." They look meticulously at sale margins and profits. To rely solely on numbers for the evaluation criteria is a monumental mistake for a coach or program administrator. Motivational coaches will augment quantitative measurements with qualitative ones such as desire, intensity, and a concentrated effort to improve and fulfill goals.

Compare Actual Results With Projected Standards

This step in the control process is the easiest to comprehend. The underlying question is, How does the actual measured performance compare to the projected performance? The most effective tool for this comparison is a performance evaluation chart. The following performance evaluation chart could be designed from our previous academic example.

Administrative Tip

The first scenario in the appraisal of a program's performance (do nothing), has a potentially perilous long-term ramification associated with it: complacency. If there is ever an option in a managerial control situation, take the challenging choice over the complacent choice, especially in significant operating areas.

Figure 2: Performance Evaluation Chart

Performance Standard	Actual Result	Variance
1. Players must attend 90% of all classes and take an active role in class participation.	A measured attendance of 86% was recorded. Player's progress reports for class participation were all positive.	<4 %> class variance.
2. 75% on mid-terms and finals.	Team average of 81% on midterms and finals. High/low range 72-96%.	+6% variance on testing.
3. 80% on term papers and 100% on homework.	64% on term papers; 78% on homework.	<17%> variance on papers and <22%> on homework.
Overall Goal: 3.0 GPA	Actual: 2.91 GPA	<.09%> overall GPA variance.

The control process is completed by evaluating the variance column on the performance evaluation chart. The evaluation can have one of three possible outcomes:

1. Do nothing—if meeting an acceptable range of variances, then do not adjust control system.
2. Correct deviation—if the variable falls outside acceptable limits, corrective action will be necessary. Positive deviations should be examined for new insights into such successes while negative deviations should be the foundations of learning.
3. Revise standard—after learning that there are certain variances, the revision of performance standards might be necessary. This, in turn, will retrack performance into achievable goals. (Bedian, 1993)

If the individual athlete or the team exceeds standards and goals, readjust the standards to an elevated level yet still make them achievable. If the team, athletes, or staff are not achieving standards:

1. Ask "why"?
2. See if the problem can be fixed.
3. Either maintain standards or readjust them to a more realistic range.

Feedback

The primary advantage of using an organized, participative control system (whether for an individual or a team) is that it provides the basis for feedback. All variances should be discussed, whether they are positive or negative. How one handles those variances is a part of one's makeup as a program administrator and leader. In Szilagy's text, *Management, and*

Performance, there are general guidelines (dos and don'ts) for discussing feedback information:

Avoid
1. Focusing on a person or personality.
2. Being judgmental.
3. Using negative terms and criticism.
4. Using "you vs. me" attitude.
5. Giving insincere and undeserved praise.
6. Dominating the performance interview.
7. Being a "nitpicker".
8. Being or appearing to be bored or hurried.

Employ
1. Focus on performance.
2. Be descriptive.
3. Reassure subordinates. . . build on strengths.
4. Use "we" when discussing negative variances in performance.
5. Be specific in examples—use performance evaluation chart.
6. Counsel—do not demand or advise.
7. Jointly summarize new performance standards for the future.

A coach or program administrator must communicate to his or her athletes and staff that even though they are ultimately accountable for their own performance results, they are part of a program and that the top priority is to help them achieve. If the coach or program administrator can instill this feeling in them and in the program, the staff and athletes will look forward to the challenges of higher performance standards rather then dreading them.

Summary

The managerial assignment of control is vital in helping with the smooth flow of program operations as well as the ultimate realization of program goals. Proper control systems isolate and solve problems, ensure quality benchmarks, monitor staff and athlete's performances, and prevent an organization from squandering its limited resources. Through the proactive application of the control process, a coach or program administrator can standardize and measure a staff member or athlete's performance while conveying essential feedback to each for improving and maximizing potential.

Administrative Tip

Throughout all aspects of the management process (and, in fact, all operational activities), aggressively scrutinize other comparable athletic programs. Simply put, if these programs are performing better than one's program, emulate them and even improve on their concepts and operations. The key to emulating these programs is in not letting one's ego block an opportunity. Get rid of ego and stubbornness. If another program's operations are superior, they are superior—PERIOD. Learn from them.

Section II ....

Internal Program Administration

Section II: Internal Program Administration

Section II is an investigation into the internal program elements of budgeting fundamentals and operational spreadsheets. Most coaches typically do not have in-depth knowledge of concepts such as accounting, finance, and budgeting. None-the-less, a working knowledge and ability to construct primary program budgets (and subsequent spreadsheets) is critical for smooth program operation.

- Chapter 6 succinctly looks into the basic concepts surrounding budget fundamentals.
- Chapter 7 details the construction of a team travel spreadsheet and the construction of a comprehensive travel itinerary.
- Appendix 7A examines academic spreadsheets.
- Appendix 7B concludes the section with an overview of scholarship spreadsheets.

Chapter 6 ....
Budgeting Fundamentals

Objectives

- To provide coaches and program administrators with a practical outline for budgeting.
- To distinguish the two types of situational budgeting: Entrepreneurial and Operating/ Expense.
- To examine the concept of operating/expense budgeting.
- To consider budgeting as a function of managerial control.

Introduction

Before a discussion of budgeting can commence, it must be emphatically stated that the process of budgeting (in most organizations) is fairly simple to understand. So why does the mere mention of the term evoke extreme mental distress for most program administrators and coaches? Three prominent reasons stand out. The first is that budgets are predictions and predictions deal with uncertainty and ambiguity. The second is that to do them accurately, budgets take time, thought, and effort. If a coach or program administrator is not detail oriented, budgeting can be an arduous process. The third is that budgets deal with a very critical and carefully scrutinized organizational resource: money. Money is the one program resource that elicits immediate attention from all organization stakeholders.

Budgeting Defined

The most comprehensive use of the term *budgeting* is exemplified by the following definition:

1. A budget is a financial plan serving as a pattern for and a control over future operations.
2. A budget is any estimate of future costs.

Administrative Tip

A coach or program administrator who has never budgeted before should not think twice about contacting a colleague with experience to request help. Budgeting takes insight as well as practice. Plunging blindly into the budgeting process can have considerable negative ramifications for the program now and in the future.

3. A budget is a systematic plan for the utilization of manpower, materials, and other resources. (Stedry,1990)

Budgets are for a specific terminal time period (ordinarily a fiscal year). While they are utilized for projecting future resource allocation, they are grounded in historical data. In other words, what is spent in previous budgetary periods will be the foundation for projections into succeeding budgetary periods. In his 1993 text, *Powerful Budgeting for Better Planning and Management*, Finney proposes some major objectives and critical benefits of budgeting. The following is a synopsis:

- Budgets provide realism, accuracy, and internal operational consistency.
- They contain useful information for management.
- Budgets should be consistent with strategies and planning to reassure stakeholders that the program is moving in an acceptable direction.
- Budgets facilitate goal setting and measurement at all levels of planning and expenditure.
- Budgets communicate quantitative resource strategies.
- Budgets are guideposts for every department.

Situational Budgeting

From coaching and program administration, budgeting can take two different forms. The first and more difficult is that the coach or program administrator is the owner of the club or team. In this case, one must budget extensively and apply detailed accounting procedures to all operations. This circumstance is similar to entrepreneurial and corporate accounting. In this type of operation, it is advisable (unless the coach has a formal accounting and business background) to employ and directly work with an accounting consultant. The consultant will help set up all of the program's financial statements, projected budgets, and year-end fiscal reports. Documents such as cash flow statements, balance sheets, and income statements (both actual and projected) are typically beyond general coaching knowledge.

The second form of budgeting is the one that is relevant for the majority of coaches: operating/expense budgeting. This is a system where the program is a part (or unit) within a whole athletic department or corporate structure. In this case, the process of financial statement generation is completed outside the program. The coach or administrator is provided with specific parameters within which the program must operate. In other words, the program's owner (in a professional setting) or the athletic administration (in a high school, junior, or senior college) stipulates a specific dollar amount for the program to operate. The projected amount can be divided into predetermined line items (recruiting, scholarships, phone, etc.) or it can be an aggregate total. In the latter case, the coach determines the allocation for the individual line items.

Administrative Tip

Consultants (such as lawyers, accountants, medical practitioners, trainers, etc.) should be considered a necessary evil if the program's operations necessitate their use. They are professional experts in their fields. While the upfront costs of specialists could be considered exorbitant, skillful consultants can pay for their services over the long term many times over. If the program cannot finance consultants on a permanent basis, hire them to set up operational systems that are as self-sustaining as is feasible.

Operating and Expense Budget

In a business, production operating budgets

> deal with costs and expenses for the goods and services produced. . . the supervisor may be told to control the cost/expenditures in the department as closely as possible and not to worry about the price charged for goods and services produced and the cost/expenses outside the department. That is, one may be told to concentrate on the costs/expenses that can be influenced and controlled. (Ramsey, 1985)

Taking this concept literally and focusing it on athletic program administration, first identify all of the program's costs. Once again, this concept is not as simple as it seems. A good place to start is with the identification of historical data. Simply put, the expense categories that the program has had in the past and present are the foundations for the future projected categories. However, this is not the end of the process. The program, through planning and goal definition, has a futuristic viewpoint that possibly is very different from its current and historical position. In this instance, discover what new possible expenditures (based on the program's mission, goals, and direction) need to be defined. The coach or program administrator needs to think this step through from every possible angle. Look at the fiscal year completely. While some of us tend to dissect our in-season expenses, never deemphasize the off-season projected expenses.

Once the program's expense categories have been determined, enter the dollar amounts that are believed to be accurate. As with budget category definitions, historical data is a good starting point in determining the dollar amount for each line-item expense. From that starting point, each expense must be looked at individually to determine operating variables from past years to present. In other words, are our operations remaining essentially the same? If so, then the utilization of historical expense information is relevant, applicable, and defendable. If we have evaluated and subsequently changed any aspect of our operation, then an increase or decrease in a line item might be warranted.

For example, if one's team is traveling to the same locations, with the same travel squad, with the same method of transportation, etc., then historical data can be used with a fairly high degree of confidence to determine our team's travel line item. Any deviations (possibly different locations, larger or smaller travel squad, etc.) imply that the line item will need to be adjusted accordingly.

Budgets as Managerial Controls

> Besides providing a valuable foundation for operations, budgets can be used as a means of management control, which involve comparing projections to actual performances and holding individuals responsible and accountable. . . use budgets like a navigation chart. . . significant deviations from budgeted

Administrative Tip

As previously stated, it takes time and reflection to budget correctly. When initiating the thinking process of operation/expense budgeting, it is advisable to

1. List all of the likely expenses (past and future).
2. Isolate all of the program's fixed expenses that will be a part of the program no matter what level of output or operation:
3. Uncover the elastic expense accounts last.

These resilient expenses are the line items that a coach or program administrator can regulate with to meet bottom-line constraints.

Administrative Tip

Think of accounting and budgeting as a way to tell the program's story through numbers. From a managerial control viewpoint, ask "Did we tell the story that we predicted we were going to?" Sometimes the stories told have happy endings and other times, unhappy ones.

Because budgets deal with the most critical and limited resource in a program, namely money, all internal stakeholders need to have a guide for operating and spending. For this reason, budgets need to be monitored continuously. A good practice is to keep an expense ledger (either by hand or by computer) that shows a program's individual line items. The line items can be broken down into fiscal budget, actual expenditures, and operational variances. Another ledger technique could be similar to one's personal checkbook, where dates and running balances show the remaining funds as well as when expenditures were incurred. Furthermore, if one can accurately maintain encumbrances against running totals, it will give a clear picture of the account. Finally, any major deviations from projected to actual spending should be narratively recorded and explained for budget review clarification at the end of the fiscal year.

Summary

Prior to a coach or program administrator embarking on the process of program budgeting, he or she needs to have a comprehensive understanding of the operational environment in which the organization functions. Entrepreneurial management and independent program budgeting differ significantly from organizational budgeting. Entrepreneurial operations need to generate complex financial statements as well as detailed reporting systems. On the other hand, organizational budgeting is the projection and tracking of expenses within a departmental structure. Organizational budgeting, in which most coaches and program administrators function, deals with a budgeting technique categorized as *expense budgeting*. Expense budgeting is

1. Identification of program expense categories.
2. Projecting the expense (if possible, with a historical perspective).
3. Tracking actual costs for each category. This tracking of expenses must be pursued with diligence and precision.

This three-step process will, in turn, supply the coach or program administrator with a true financial picture of the program.

Chapter 7 ....
Travel Spreadsheets

Objectives

- To explain the essential principles of travel budgeting.
- To present a graphic travel spreadsheet template.
- To clarify the make-up and calculations behind each categorical section of a travel spreadsheet.
- To justify the critical managerial cost control of travel spreadsheets.
- To outline the rationale behind constructing a travel itinerary.
- To provide a model framework for the content and design of a comprehensive travel itinerary.

Introduction

This chapter reviews a primary area of sports management operational budgeting: team travel. The section provides information for the construction of a travel worksheet as well as some general tips on budgeting and team travel. The chapter concludes with functional uses of travel worksheets as a cost control instrument.

Basic Principles of Travel Budgeting

The following are some underlying fundamentals to travel budgeting:

1. As with all types of operational budgeting, in advance, clarify if the organization uses a deductive or inductive budgeting philosophy. Deductive budgeting is deriving conclusions from a known amount. Simply put, there is a certain bottom-line dollar amount for the specific budget and the coach or program administrator must work within that amount (backward flow). Inductive budgeting (or zero-

A coach or program administrator should, at all times, associate two concepts with program travel. The first is organization. One can never be too organized when it comes to team and program travel. The second is responsibility. A coach or program administrator is always held accountable for all facets of the trip (even if he or she is not physically present). By committing to memory these two salient (and sometimes frightening) ideas, a coach or program administrator will be motivated to decrease or eliminate unpleasant travel situations and quandaries.

Administrative Tip

Quotes can be use to get enhanced services at reduced costs. Play travel companies against one another. It is not unscrupulous but a straight-forward fact of the competitive economy in which all businesses function. If a coach or program administrator consents to a higher quote without investigating other options, then he or she will have no one to blame when resources at a later point are constricted. The more money one saves by receiving superior prices (without forfeiting safety and quality), the more money the program will have to disburse in other areas.

based budgeting) is operating forward through each category and line item without targeted bottom-line constraints. In other words, inductive, zero-based budgeting would have the coach calculating all of the trips' total expenses and reporting back to the program's administrators what the "bottom line" would be for travel.

2. Use actual quotes whenever possible. If quotes are unattainable, use historical price range estimates. It is advisable when using estimates to "go high" on all calculations and costs. When getting quotes, remember to ask for inclusive prices (i.e., prices that include taxes, fees, etc.). Another sound tip is to get written confirmations whenever possible.

3. Stay consistent with the format and calculations from line item to line item and category to category. Any deviations from the norm must be explained in a supplementary document. Remember, it is substantially easier to justify the numbers if assumptions are applied consistently throughout the travel budget.

4. Personally triple-check all calculations. Then have a program staff member also verify accuracy of calculations. Remember, it is easier to justify numbers to administrators if they are accurate and stand up to scrutiny.

5. When getting quotes, get three different assessments. If using an outside agent or consultant, insist that they procure three quotes.

6. Standardize the budgetary process by designing and utilizing budget spreadsheets. The design of a budget worksheet will be dictated by the type of information required, the depth of information required, and the durational period of information required.

Travel Worksheets

The following chart is a traditional travel worksheet. Each category (column) will be explained briefly.

Destination: This line is self-explanatory. In addition to city destination, incorporate actual trip dates. For a more coherent worksheet, keep the program's trips in chronological order from first trip to last.

# of Days: The critical importance of this category is that it will be utilized for other line-item calculations. Depending on the budget and monetary circumstance, this category could be broken down into 1/4, 1/2, or whole days. The more detailed the daily breakdown, the more precise (and unfortunately, inflexible) the dollar amounts. Days should be measured from departure time (at point of origin) to projected time of arrival (back at point of origin). For example, the departure time could be noon on Thursday with an estimated arrival time of Sunday at 6:00 p.m. In this instance, the coach or program administrator could classify this trip as 4 whole days, 3 1/2 days, or 3 1/4 days.

# of People: Another influential category for other line-item calculations is the number of people in the travel squad. A standardized travel squad would simplify the work associated with this item.

Figure 1: Travel Spreadsheets

Destination	# Days	# People	Meals	Lodging	Air	Charter	Van	Gas	Other	Total

Meals: Meals can be computed by using two distinct methods. One could adopt a flat rate method or a per-meal cost. The following are examples:

Flat Rate
3 ? days x 20 people x $22.00 per day = $1540.00 Total Meals

Per Meal
Meals - Breakfast $5.00
Lunch $7.00
Dinner $10.00

In a 3 ? day trip, the program could have four team breakfasts, four lunches, and three dinners. The calculations:

Breakfast—$5.00 x 4 total breakfasts x 20 people =	$400.00
Lunch—$7.00 x 4 total lunches x 20 people =	$560.00
Dinner—$10.00 x 3 total dinners x 20 people =	$600.00
Total Meals	$1560.00

Lodging: The number of rooms needed by the group is solely dependent on the team travel squad and the program's policy on how many players and staff to a room. An example of the room calculation is as follows:

20 people/2 to a room = 10 rooms

10 rooms x $55.00 per room x 3 nights = $1650.00

Furnish hotels with the travel rooming list as early as possible so they can block rooms in the same general area in the hotel. Furthermore, get confirmations and contractual arrangements in writing. It is strongly recommended to (1) get firm price quotes and (2) subsequent reservations as soon as it is practical in the worksheet process. Most hotels function on the supply and demand principle. Conventions, athletic events, and city functions can decrease availability, which increases price.

The next four categories are directly related to team transportation.

Air: If the program's transportation mandates air travel, then it is a matter of choice whether one uses a travel agent to make the arrangements or does it oneself. Some essential fundamentals if deciding to engage a travel agent are as follows:

1. Make sure the travel agent is a Certified Travel Counselor (CTC). CTCs are accredited travel agents that have at least 5 years of experience and have fulfilled all course requirements stipulated by the Institute of Certified Travel Agents.

2. Comparison shop. One method of comparison shopping for travel agents would be to write up the general criteria for airline travel (and other inclusive services such as vans) and then forward it to at least three different travel agents. Some of the travel specifications could include dates and times, places, ground transportation, etc. Select the most competitive, cost-efficient, and time-effective travel service.

3. Once a choice is made of an agency, deal exclusively with one agent. This will eliminate miscommunications, duplications, and omissions.

4. Secure a direct billing system with the travel agent to expedite payments and ticket distribution.

5. With the travel agent, lock in rates as early as possible. If feasible, keep group size 15 people or more to qualify for group rates.

The basic worksheet calculation for air travel is as follows:

# of travelers x ticket price (tax included) = total ticket price

Charter: Any seasoned traveler will testify that not all charter bus lines are the same. If traveling by bus, it is strongly recommended to comparative shop at least five bus line companies. Likewise, get recommendations from other knowledgeable groups or teams that travel by bus.

The distance to be traveled, the size of the bus needed, and days and times of charter service are the three elements that will determine quoted prices. Three important considerations in acquiring a charter company:

1. While airline tickets represent contractual arrangements between traveler and airline, charter companies deal with nonconforming quotes. Get a written contractual agreement from the bus line that expressly itemizes dates, times, size of vehicle, pickup and drop-off locales, and costs.

2. Specifically inquire if the contractual agreement includes bus driver fees and room costs. Some companies will defray the bus driver's accommodations and miscellaneous expenses, while others will have the coach include them in the program's traveling costs.

3. Most bus line companies operate on a prepaid basis only. However, deposits can hold reservations.

From a worksheet perspective, there are no calculations associated with the charter category.

Vans: There are two instances that necessitate utilizing van transportation. One, if vans are the program's primary mode of transportation (local trips) and two, for local around-town transportation if the program has traveled by air. A few salient recommendations concerning van travel: For teams, acquire 15-passenger vehicles if they are at all accessible. These vans are typically more cost effective and substantially more spacious than other rental vehicles. Remember, not only are vans transporting players and staff, but often their bulky luggage. An unfortunate problem associated with 15-passenger vans is their limited availability (especially in smaller markets). In addition, van travel for athletic teams and programs over the past few years has come under serious scrutiny by governing organizations as well as internal administrators. Once again, secure reservations and subsequent confirmations early in the worksheet process.

Contact major rental companies (Budget, Hertz, etc.) or car/truck dealerships in destination locales. From a cost standpoint, rental companies operate on a daily basis with a half hour to an hour grace period. If planning van transportation with this in mind, extra day charges might be avoided. Furthermore, always check for unlimited mileage status on all rentals. Reminder, all drivers must be at least 25 years old. The program

Administrative Tip

As soon as possible, reinforce a positive employer-subordinate relationship with the trip's bus driver. If the drive does not have one, review with him or her the trip's itinerary and targeted timelines. Neglecting to involve a bus driver could have profound travel consequences.

must secure all rentals with a major credit card and the optional insurance coverage is solely up to the organization's policy on additional insurance.

The basic worksheet calculation:

# of vans x # of days x inclusive cost per vehicle = total van costs

An addition to this calculation could be the possibility of excess miles over and above the free rental miles.

Gas: The assessments for gas consumption needs to be consistent throughout the worksheet. Gas costs are estimated from a projected trip mileage vantage. A reasonable rule of thumb for fuel consumption:

Vans—10 miles per gallon

Large cars—15 miles per gallon

Small cars—20 miles per gallon

Cost calculation—Total estimated trip mileage/Miles per gallon = Total gas consumption per vehicle

Total gas per vehicle x # of vehicles = Total estimated gas consumption for trip

Total estimated gas consumption for trip x Current market rate = Total gas cost

Example:

250 total estimated miles for trip

$1.40 per gallon

2 Vans

250/10 = 25 x 2 = 50 x $1.40 = $70.00 Total cost

Other: This is the category otherwise known as *miscellaneous funds.* This reserve could be used for any unforeseen and surprise expenses as well as an overflow account to cover any underestimated items throughout spreadsheets. Calculate this amount on a daily basis.

Daily misc. amount x # of days = Total other

Spreadsheet Summary

Totaling the spreadsheet horizontally will give a per trip cost and, vertically, a per-category cost for the travel season. If the addition is accurate, the bottom right axis calculation should act as the proof for the worksheet.

The worksheet has an ultimate, critical program cost control function. Using a blank worksheet throughout the season, record actual, verifiable category expenditures for each trip. When the season is completed, use the actual expenditure worksheet to compare with the original budgeted worksheet to identify and evaluate variances. It is also advisable to use a third worksheet to document each variance. The analysis of these variances will be utilized for corrections on future budgets.

Travel Itineraries

The first question that arises when discussing travel itineraries: Why make one? There are numerous, salient reasons to compile the team's travel into a comprehensive travel itinerary packet. The following are just a few:

1. The most important reason for a comprehensive travel itinerary is group contact and accessibility. If an emergency situation occurs and it is imperative that the group be found, a detailed itinerary will accomplish this.
2. It keeps all internal stakeholders (staff and players) on the same page. Never underestimate the importance of team travel organization. A clear and precise travel itinerary will help the group avoid any potential disasters from miscommunication.
3. It keeps external stakeholders (owners, administrators, parents, etc.) informed of all team actions. This, in turn, helps avoid an otherwise endless stream of questions from the program stakeholders about where the program is and what it is doing.
4. It conveys an image of professionalism.

The format and design of the travel itinerary is entirely up to one's own preference. However, the following information should be included no matter what the design.

Trip Number: Identify each trip by number. Keep the travel itinerary in numerical order with each trip number corresponding to ascending trip dates. For example, trip number one's dates could be Sept. 1-3; trip number two's trip dates could be Sept. 10-12; etc.

Trip Dates: Self-explanatory.

Trip Location(s): Each itinerary page should be headed also by trip location(s).

Competition Times and Locations: List all relevant competition times and locations on trip.

Practice Times and Locations: List all relevant practice times and locations on trip.

Departure Time: From point of origin (predetermined site).

Arrival Times: All relevant estimated arrival times throughout trip.

Flight Information: All exact flight information including airline, flight number, flight departure time, gate of departure (if possible), and projected departure and arrival times.

Accommodations: Hotel name, address, phone, and contact name. Additionally, a confirmation number could be included as a precaution against misfiling.

Bus Line: Include the name of the bus line, the contact's name, and phone number.

Miscellaneous Information: Any additional special information that will provide the reader with unusual trip particulars.

Summary

The significance of proper travel budgeting techniques and travel itineraries can not be overstated. Travel spreadsheets organize the entire array of program travel information from a financial standpoint. Internally, travel spreadsheets furnish a fiscal focus and accountability for the program. Externally, travel spreadsheets convey fiscal responsibility and professional-

Administrative Tip

Think of the program's travel itinerary first and foremost as a safety component. Copy all parties associated with the program even if they have only a minor role in the program. One will never know who could be of assistance in case of an emergency.

Administrative Tip

Team travel, as much as any component in an athletic program, sets the climate for the organization, not only from a sense of efficiency and orderliness but from a class standpoint. Athletes and staff value quality in travel arrangements. As illogical as it may seem, while cutting trip costs may be fiscally sensible, it can lead to mediocre performances. Find out what the team's travel expectations are and, if possible financially, meet those standards. If the program can not monetarily meet athlete and staff travel criteria, be open and honest with the group and explain the program's travel limitations.

ism. They constitute an outstanding program cost-management tool. Itineraries, which are derived from spreadsheets, spell out to all parties the details of all the program's trips. It should be reiterated that travel organization, through travel itineraries, is a considerable component of smooth and safe program operations.

Appendix 7A: Academic Spreadsheets

While academic spreadsheets are not monetary, they are quantitative documents that track academic status and progress. In any sports program that operates under an educational institution, it is imperative that academic progress be monitored and controlled. This spreadsheet is an excellent tool for monitoring scholarly progress. The following is a breakdown of its components:

The top-most section should be for the title of the document. Obviously, program identification and semester or quarter delineation is the first element of the form.

Name: last name first, then first name followed by middle initial. This section should have the exact spelling of the athletes' name, so the athletes can be tracked accurately throughout the program, athletic department, and university or school. Institution Identification: This column is another tracking element unique to each student athlete. If the program's institution uses a separate and distinct student identification number that is universal throughout the school system, use that number instead.

Year: This column signifies the academic status of the athlete in years. It should be noted that it is possible in some situations to have an incongruous athletic eligibility status in years compared to an academic status in years (for example, fifth-year seniors).

The next four columns relate to the overall academic condition of each athlete for his or her academic career.

Cumulative Hours Attempted/Cumulative Hours Earned: These two columns show the number of credits (semester, quarter, etc.) taken and successfully completed. Each academic institution will have its own criteria for credits earned.

Cumulative Quality Points/Cumulative Grade Point Average: These two columns represent the total number of grade points earned and an athlete's grade point average. The total number of grade points (or in this case cumulative quality points) is calculated for each course's grade times the number of credits for that course. For example, in a 4.0 grade point system, the following is a breakdown of points per grade:

A = 4 Quality Points
B = 3 Quality Points
C = 2 Quality Points
D = 1 Quality Points
F = 0 Quality Points

Simply take the corresponding quality points earned times the credits for that class. If a student athlete achieved a B in a three-credit course, his or her total quality points earned for that class would be nine. To arrive at the cumulative amount, just add up all of their total class quality points. To arrive at a cumulative grade point average, just take the total credit hours earned and divide that into total cumulative quality points.

Semester Hours Attempted/Semester Hours Earned: These two columns deal with the present academic semester.

Semester Quality Points/Semester Grade Point Average: These two columns are a microcosm of the total columns (cumulative quality points and cumulative grade point average). Their calculation formulas are the same as the cumulative columns, but are solely based on the current semester results.

Academic Status: This is a narrative description of the student athlete's progress and status. Descriptions can range from Magna, Summa, Cum Laude as well as good, warning, and dismissal.

Learning Lab Hours: This final column deals with learning lab/study hall hours due for each student athlete. Typically these hours are determined by prior academic performance.

Figure 1 Academic Spreadsheet provided by:

Georgia State University Athletic Association
Senior Women's Administrator/Senior Associate Athletic Director
Carol Cohen

Figure 2: Academic Spreadsheet

Name	SS#	Yr.	Cum. Hrs. Attemp.	Cum. Hrs. Earned	Cum. Qual. Pts.	Cum. GPA	Sem. Hrs. Attemp	Sem. Hrs. Earned	Sem. Qual. Pts.	Sem. GPA	Academic Status	Regents R/W	LL Hours

Appendix 7B: Scholarship Spreadsheets

Spreadsheets can be utilized for numerous internal operational items. Their graphic depiction and situational appropriateness is limited only by the program elements being examined. One program element that works well with a spreadsheet is athletic program scholarships. The following chart is an example of how colleges (both two-year and four-year institutions) can utilize this document.

Athlete's Name: List the athlete's full name including middle name if any.

Identification Number: List the institution's identification number for each student athlete (either social security or specific assigned identification number). This will be the tracking record for each student athlete.

Year of Eligibility: Identify the upcoming academic and athletic status year of each athlete.

In State, Out of State, or International: Delineate each student athlete's residential status.

Tuition: List the dollar amount awarded.

On-Campus Housing: List the dollar amount for student athletes living in university housing.

Off-Campus Housing: If the student athletes are allowed to live off-campus, list any cash supplements for off-campus living arrangements.

Meals/Books: Dollar amount awarded.

Total: Individualized totals for each student athlete. These totals are used to cross-check any other scholarship documentation.

Comments: Pertinent supplementary information individualized for each student athlete.

Figure 3: Scholarship Spreadsheet

Athlete Name	I.D. Number	Year of Eligibility	In-State/Out of State	Tuition Intl.	On-Campus Housing	Off Campus Housing	Meals	Books	Misc.	Totals	Comments

Section III ....
Marketing Concepts

Section III: Marketing Concepts

The concept of program marketing is one of the most critical and (unfortunately) underutilized in athletic administration. This section not only encompasses the foundations of marketing, but also elaborates on specific tools available in putting together the program's marketing plan.

- Chapter 8 embraces fundamental marketing concepts such as environmental scanning, the marketing environment, customer behavior, market segmentation, and target market selection.
- Appendix 8A provides a format for a structured marketing plan.
- Chapter 9 examines promotional tools as well as the concept of marketing communication.
- Chapter 10 looks specifically at public relations for sports programs.
- Appendix 10A outlines news releases.

Chapter 8 ....
Marketing Fundamentals

Objectives

- To present a comprehensive assessment of the marketing concept as it relates to athletic program administration.
- To elucidate the six external environmental forces that affect all business organizations as well as athletic programs.
- To provide an in-depth breakdown of the marketing mix/4 Ps of marketing.
- To consider sports program product and service development through a structured six-step process.
- To convey the central pricing models of price elasticity and pricing objectives and goals.
- To furnish the fundamentals of athletic program product and service distribution.
- To impart a foundational definition for marketing communication and promotion.
- To examine customer behavior through a detailed five-step consumer-decision process.
- To analyze market segmentation from the perspective of geography, demography, psychographics, diversity, behaviors, and benefits sought.

Administrative Tip

Marketing college and professional sports is in many ways different from high school and entrepreneurial sports marketing. College and professional marketing is characteristically delegated to an independent marketing director or department, while in high school and entrepreneurial sports situations, the coach or program administrator is accountable for all facets of marketing. A viable solution for high school, entrepreneurial clubs, and college and professional athletic programs with insufficient marketing support is the enlistment of college student interns. The financial outlay for these interns is negligible because their pay is college credits earned for work provided. However, this strategy has two inherent problems. The first is that the associations with an intern are customarily as long as the semester lasts (and the credits are earned), and the second drawback is that the quality of work can vary greatly from student to student and from school to school.

Introduction

Marketing is an organizational discipline that interfaces with almost all of the program's functions. Even beyond that, marketing can control a majority of the program's operational components. The term *marketing* is probably the most misused and misinterpreted word in today's business world. The first impression that one associates with marketing is advertising. The function of advertising is just one facet of the total concept of marketing. Marketing also involves product selection, customer research, distribution of the product, pricing decisions, and numerous other administrative elements.

Marketing Defined

Administrative Tip

The American Marketing Association (www.ama.org) is a tremendous resource for marketing information and educational options.

The American Marketing Association (AMA) defines marketing as "the process of planning and executing the concept of pricing, promotion, and distribution of goods, ideas, and services to create exchanges that satisfy individual and organizational goals" (Pride and Ferrel, 1993). This definition has three major elements:

1. Formation of products and services, pricing, distribution, and promotion (also known as the marketing mix or the 4 Ps of marketing).
2. Behavior and satisfaction of individuals and customers.
3. Marketing planning process (see Appendix 8A).

The goal of this chapter is to dissect and explain these three primary elements of marketing as they relate to our profession of coaching and athletic program administration.

Overall Marketing Environment

An assessment of the program's overall marketing environment must proceed the three focal components of the AMA's definition. Essentially, the practical application of business marketing consists of taking the program's internal product or service and selling it externally. In other words, marketing facilitates exchanges between the organization and its current and potential clientele. However, prior to engaging in an exchange, one will need to be familiar with how the marketing environment will affect that exchange.

Figure 1 is an illustration of the marketing concept and how outside environmental factors affect it.

A clarification of the illustration is as follows:

Athletic Program's Operation and Marketing Mix

The far left boxes denote the particular sports program and the product that it produces for an exchange. The marketing mix (4 Ps) details how the coach/program administrator is going to conceive, price, distribute, and promote the product that the program produces.

Exchanges

Administrative Tip

Exchanges deal with value provided by the athletic program for value given by the supporters. Value furnished by the program's supporters goes beyond money. Value bestowed by supporters can include time, convenience, mental exertion, and psychological energy.

The formation of an exchange means that people give up something in order to receive something else that they would rather have . . . typically money for goods and services. Five conditions must be satisfied for an exchange to take place:

1. There must be at least two parties.
2. Each party must have something of value to the other party.

Figure 1: Marketing Concept and the Environment (broadly adapted from Lamb, Hair, and McDaniel, 1992)

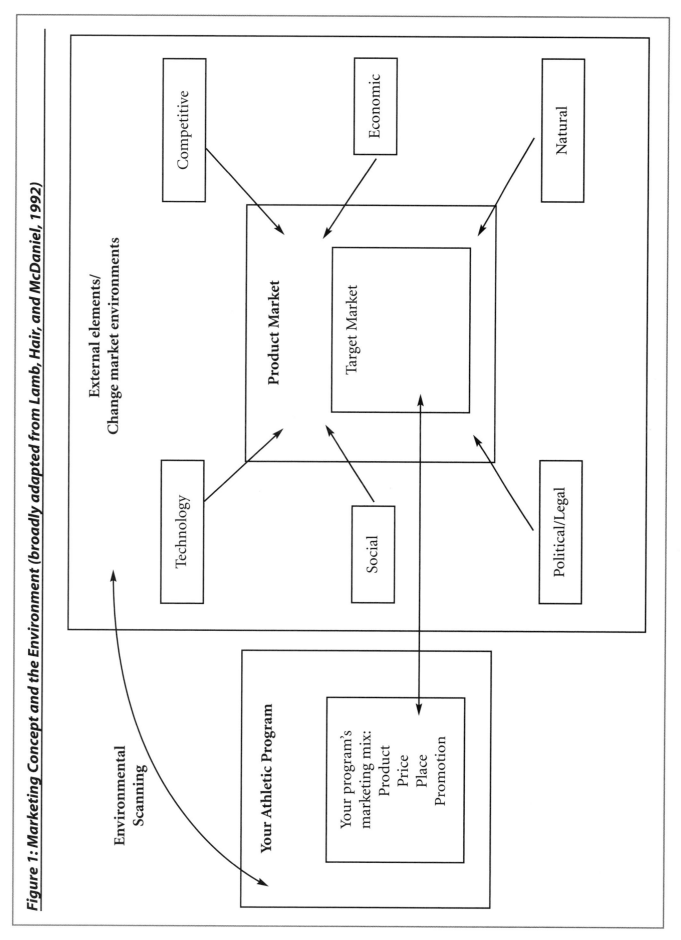

3. Each party must be able to communicate with the other party and deliver the goods and services that the other party desires.
4. Each party must be free to accept or reject the offer.
5. Each party must believe that it is appropriate or desirable to deal with the other party. (Lamb, Hair, and McDaniel, 1992)

The concept of exchanges is at the heart of all business actions. Exchanges deal with benefits and perceptions. In other did, does the consumer experience a positive benefit (tangible, social, personal, or sensory) and did that exchange provide a "value for value" trade? If so, the consumer will seek out that exchange again. If not, then the service or product in need will be purchased elsewhere.

Product and Target Markets

A market is "an aggregate group of people who have needs for products in a product class and who have the ability, willingness, and authority to purchase such products" (Pride and Ferrel, 1993). A target market is merely a group of people inside a market with even more explicit attributes upon which a business (in our case an athletic program) converges all of its marketing effort. For example, the all-encompassing market for athletic programs is entertainment. One can then break down the broad market classification of entertainment into the more detailed (but still sizeable) category of sports entertainment. From there, dissect the sports entertainment market into the precise target market of sports entertainment customers for a specific sport, in a particular geographic area, with a distinct income level, etc. The more clear-cut the target market, the more systematic and coherent the program's marketing efforts. This topic will be elaborated in the discussion of market segmentation.

Environmental Scanning

The six external environmental factors that must be continuously monitored by an athletic program are technology, competition, natural, social, economic, and political/legal. These six factors will affect how the product (or in our case, sports program entertainment) is perceived, accepted, and desired by the program's target market. The six factors are discussed below.

Technology Factor

Administrative Tip

When scanning the environment for the influential external component of technology, only review relevant current and future technologies that will influence the program. Do not spend time on technological advancements that will have little or no impact on the program.

The first environmental factor that the coach or program administrator should examine is technology. There is virtually no business that is not profoundly affected by the accelerating volume of technology. Sports programs are no exception. Computerization, cell phones, advanced training systems, and the Internet are just a small number of technological advancements that need consideration. The technological investigation should focus not only on currently available technology but also on how projected technological advancements may affect the program's operations in the future.

Competition Factor

Another influential external environmental factor that needs monitoring is competition. To do this, the coach or program administrator must assemble what in the business world is called a competitive analysis. In their 1994 text, *Essentials of Marketing*, McCarthy and Perreault design an indispensable framework for competitive analysis. Figure 2 presents an adaptation of their concept.

Figure 2: Framework for Competitive Analysis (McCarthy and Perreault, 1994)

	Firm's Current or Planned Strategy	Competitor #1 Strengths and Weaknesses	Competitor #2 Strengths and Weaknesses
Target Market			
Product			
Price			
Place			
Promotion			
Competitive Barriers			
Competitive Responses			

An elaboration of the chart is as follows:

Columns—The first column is the program's unique competitive position and strategy while the next two columns are the direct competitors' positions. Each section going down the column is centered on the perception of a tactic or plan as a strategic strength (+) or a weakness (-).

Rows—There are seven separate areas (rows) in which to register what the program is doing (strength/weakness) and what the competition is doing (strength/weakness).

Target market is fundamentally who the program and its competition are focusing marketing efforts on.

Product, **price**, **place**, and **promotion** describe how the program and its competition are internally conceiving, pricing, distributing, and promoting that product.

Administrative Tip

When calculating competition, support suppositions and opinions with as much tangible quantitative information as possible. Combining compelling insight with hard data will yield a more accurate picture of the program's opponents.

Competitive barriers "are conditions that make it difficult, or even impossible, for a program or the program's competition to compete in that market. Such barriers may limit one's own plans or, alternatively, block competitor's responses to an innovative strategy" (McCarthy and Perreault, 1994).

The **competitive response** category is the projected strategies and tactics the program and its competition will take to counterbalance each other's strengths and weaknesses.

Nature Factor

For most sports programs, the natural environment might not be as consequential an environmental factor to scrutinize as the other five external factors. Obviously, sports programs that are outdoors need to address geographical weather patterns, pollution, and other possible environmental concerns that could affect marketing activities.

Social Factors

The factor of the social environment is defined as

> the people in a society and their values, beliefs, and behaviors… [M]arketers describe this environment in terms of who the people are (their ages, incomes, hometowns, and so forth) and the characteristics of their culture. (Churchill and Peter, 1998)

From this designation, the leading questions that surface for sports programs:

1. How does society view our sport and program and what marketing opportunities are possible from this perspective?
2. Are there subcultures that are more interested in our sport and program?
3. Does society expect our sport and program to act in a socially responsible way?

Economic Factor

The economic environment deals with a region's/nation's purchasing power and its discretionary income. An economic environment that is stable or growing has stronger purchasing power. The stronger the purchasing power, the higher the discretionary spending. This presents numerous marketing opportunities. Conversely, the poorer the economic situation in a certain city, region, or nation, the less the purchasing power and discretionary spending. A climate of economic downturn and recession presents significant marketing concerns for sports programs whose "life blood" is based on unencumbered discretionary spending.

Political/Legal Factor

The political/legal factor in environmental scanning is the legislation affecting one's program operation. From a sports standpoint, athletic programs have two tiers of legislation to identify and monitor. The first is our governmental legislation that all businesses have to recognize and comply with. Examples of this can range from the IRS to the INS to the EEOC. The sec-

Administrative Tip

Economic examinations should be in line with contingency or scenario analysis. Simply put, evaluate the economic impact on the program of both ideal economic conditions and depressed economic affairs.

Administrative Tip

Always maintain the most recent sports-specific legislative materials for referencing. Maintain a file of legislative changes by the sports lawmaking body throughout the year.

ond tier is the particular sport's governing body and its regulatory legislation. The concentration and intensity of regulations, bylaws, and directives are sports specific as well as level specific (e.g., NCAA, NAIA, professional).

The Marketing Mix: 4 Ps of Marketing

After the external marketing environmental scanning, a coach or program administrator should consider the internal marketing process known as the marketing mix or 4 Ps of marketing. In the business world, Hisrich has defined the marketing mix as

> all the controllable marketing elements of the firm available for use in customer satisfaction. These controllable marketing elements which comprise a firm's offering can be classified in four areas. . . product, price, distribution/place, and promotion.
> Product: The product area includes all aspects of the physical product or service being offered for sale. . . . [D]ecisions need to be made on quality, assortment, breadth and depth of product line, warrantees/guarantees, service, etc.
> Pricing: The price of the product/service drastically influences whether or not it will be purchased and the image of the product/service. . . . [I]t should take into account the three C's of pricing - cost, competition, and the consumer.
> Place: Distribution covers two different areas. . . . [F]irst the channels of distribution, which are the institutions that handle the product between the firm and the consumer. . . and the second area deals with the aspect of physically moving the product.
> Promotion: Involves policies and procedures relating to four areas: personal selling, advertising, sales promotions, and publicity. (Hisrich, 1990)

Kotler (1994) analyzes the 4 Ps in further detail. Figure 3 is an adaptation of his concepts.

All four of these marketing elements play a role in sports programs. However, sports programs produce services that have entertainment value rather than actual tangible products. "Services have four unique characteristics that distinguish them from goods: intangibility, inseparability, heterogeneity, and perishability" (Lamb, Hair, and McDaniel, 1992). The characteristics are explained here.

As stated earlier, sports programs are in the entertainment market. Athletic programs are commodities that are consumed via spectator participation and fan involvement. They do not generate a tangible product. The inseparability of a service refers to the concept that the consumer is using a service at the same time as he or she pays for the service. In other words, the fan is present during the delivery of the entertainment. The characteristic of heterogeneity refers to the fact that while products can be very similar (if not precisely alike) services such as sports performance are distinct and dynamic. Finally, services such as sports entertainment are perishable because they are time specific. Once a performance is over, a consumer can

Figure 3: The Four Ps of Marketing (adapted from Kotler, 1994)

Marketing Mix

Product	**Price**
Product Variety	List Price
Design	Discounts
Quality	Allowances
Features	Payments
Brand Name	Credit Terms
Packaging	
Sizes	
Services	
Warranties	
Returns	

Target Market

Place	**Promotion**
Channels	Sales Promos
Coverage	Advertising
Assortment	Sales Force
Locations	Public Relations
Inventory	Direct Marketing

Administrative Tip

When attempting to conceive a new program product and service, at all costs avoid gimmicks and publicity stunts that will damage the integrity of the athletic program. While these marketing techniques will direct short-term attention to the product and program, their long-term effects could be irreparable. Uniqueness and a high-class reputation will bring extended growth.

never see it again in present time. With this distinction between services and products given, we can definitively adapt the marketing mix concept to athletic programs.

Product/Service/Output/Performance

As program administrators, the chief and foremost concern is with the product (in our case, athletic performance). Inside that theme, there should be an unconditional single-mindedness quality and value. Quality can relate to an athletic program's performance, presentation, facilities, operational administration, and any other aspects that directly or indirectly influence its output. Without quality, marketing and promotions break down.

Another product/service issue relates to the uniqueness of one's athletic program. Uniqueness is used to separate the program from its competition and to confirm and sustain the image of the program in the mind of the customers and supporters. Uniqueness is the strategic concept of differentiation that is reviewed in Chapter 13.

Another major marketing product/service consideration that affects sports programs is the selection of the type of products and services the program is currently offering and which products and services it is going to accentuate in the future. Some programs may be, at a given point in time, restricted to emphasizing base products or services. Lack of resources, inadequate staffing, and insufficient stakeholder cooperation are a few of the reasons to contemplate a single service marketing strategy. However, in most cases, our programs have capabilities to mature beyond the base products of performance and competition. Expanding the service into instruction, merchandising, and new athletic endeavors is just one way to diversify.

To develop new products/services, one should follow a step-by-step process that generates ideas and appraises their feasibility. Figure 4 is a graphic depiction of that process.

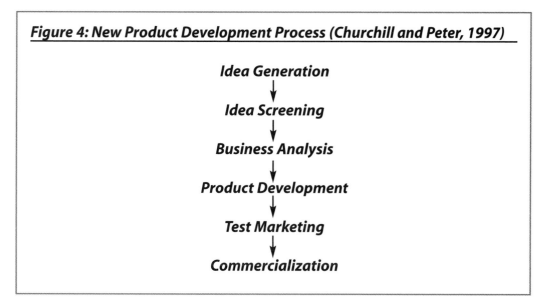

Figure 4: New Product Development Process (Churchill and Peter, 1997)

Idea Generation

Idea Screening

Business Analysis

Product Development

Test Marketing

Commercialization

Step 1: Idea Generation

Idea generation is the origination of new, relevant ideas for expanding, improving, or developing new products and services. Idea generation can happen through various avenues, such as formal requests, informal conversations, brainstorming, etc.

Step 2: Idea Screening

This stage takes the aggregate list of new ideas from Step 1 and "weeds out" all the notions, thoughts, and conceptions that are inappropriate for the program. Idea Screening, like Idea Generation, is typically qualitative and subjective in nature. The coach or program administrator and the program staff's expert opinions are customarily the determining factors. In a formal or informal setting, the coach and staff will "talk through" each new product idea to gauge its merits and appropriateness for the program now, and more notably, in the future.

Step 3: Business Analysis

This phase involves a more quantitative analysis of the program's capabilities and resources. The analysis is performed in order to determine the feasibility of an idea. Resources include the program's capital and financial situation, building and facilities, and other tangible assets that it possesses

Administrative Tip

In the preliminary stage for idea screening, it is always critical to keep current and potential supporters in mind. Their enthusiasm is a notable predictor of whether a new product and service will work. In others words, ask if the idea will generate value and benefits for present supporters and expected future supporters.

and can utilize to help realize new product ideas. Capabilities include the program members' intangible skills and knowledge. These are some of the questions asked in the business analysis stage:

- Does the idea fit our program's overall mission?
- Do we have the finances to pursue this new service or product idea?
- Will we in the future have the finances (or potential to raise the funds) to pursue this new service or product?
- Does our current building or facility have the ability to support this new idea?
- Does the idea have the potential to generate profits?
- Will there be additional labor associated with the new idea? If so, how will that affect our current personnel structure and budget?
- Do we have the technical and logistical knowledge to pursue and realize this idea?

The list of the questions is extensive. Logically, the more detailed the questions asked and the more that is and becomes known about the proposed idea, the less chance of poorer decisions and failure.

Step 4: Product/Service Development

After an idea has been probed and scrutinized and determined to be desirable and feasible, the next phase is product development. For tangible products, this step necessitates that engineering and production experts come up with a prototype of the product. Unfortunately, with the exception of merchandising, sports programs deal with intangible services, so the best that a coach or program administrator can do is put together a comprehensive plan for the new sports service. In essence, the service plan is a complete, step-by-step written amplification of what the new service (instructional camp, athletic endeavor, etc.) is about. It must be reiterated that since we are unable to visualize and hold this intangible service, the service plan must be as comprehensive and as carefully delineated as possible. The service plan is at the core of the next step: test marketing.

Step 5: Test Marketing

> Test marketing is characterized as placing a product for sale in one or more selected areas and observing its performance. . . the purpose of the test is to evaluate the product and pretest the firm's marketing plan prior to full scale introduction of the product. (Evan and Berman, 1984)

From a sports program vantage, testing out a new service concept has notable advantages. Test marketing allows program members to observe how the consumers react to a new idea or concept in authentic, real-world situations.

Such real-world testing is critical to determine

1. Whether an alteration in the sport's service is necessary.
2. Whether modifications are needed to make the new program product or service more desirable for customers and fans.

3. Whether a new idea should be scrapped rather than moved into full production.

Testing should be done on a cost-sensitive and timely basis. Additionally, open discussions or surveys of customers should be employed in conjunction with customer participation and sales testing efforts.

Step 6: Commercialization

The final section in the new product development process is commercialization. Plainly stated, this is the "go for it" stage where one has appraised and tested the idea and found it to be a sound proposition. At this point, commit the program's allotted resources to producing this new service. Effective utilization of steps one to five will decrease the possibility of concept failure. Will it remove the possibility of failure completely? No. However, implementing the stages will give the program the optimum opportunity for launching a new and successful sports product/service.

Pricing

Now that there is a viable, desired product or service (whether a recognized, conventional one or an innovative concept), one will need to price it for maximization of profits while still maintaining and increasing the program's customer base. The most lucid, rational definition of product/service pricing comes from Schewe and Hiam's 1998 book, *The Portable M.B.A. in Marketing*. They assert that the key to determining the product's price lies in understanding the value that the customer places on that product. When the price is higher than the perceived value, the exchange will not take place. Comprehending the intricacies of pricing a product (or in our case a sports service) is beyond the scope of this book. However, by understanding the central concepts of pricing, a program administrator or coach can be more conscious, in general, of pricing decisions and how they can affect the sports program.

Price Elasticity

Price elasticity is a concept that connects changes in price with changes in demand. Specifically, price elasticity reveals how sensitive the change in demand for a service is when there is a change in price for the service. If the service is elastic, then adjustments in price produce radical swings in the number of people who want it. For example, assume that the price being charged to attend one of the program's sporting events is $5.00 per ticket. Assume further that at the $5.00 level the attendance is at 1000 fans. The price would be considered elastic if an increase in the cost by $1.00 is associated with the program losing 500 fans. In this case, a 20% increase in price yields a 50% decrease in attendance. This example shows high price elasticity. Using the same example, once again the ticket price is increased from $5.00 to $6.00, but the decrease in fans from 1000 to 950. This situation is known as inelastic demand. A 20% change in price results in only a 5% decrease in fans. There is also a premise known as unitary demand. This is when a percentage change in price furnishes an exact percentage change in

Administrative Tip

A coach or program administrator can use psychological pricing techniques to modify and manipulate prices. Some psychological techniques can encompass prestige pricing (setting an elevated price to transmit an aura of high quality), odd-even pricing (which is pricing an item to make the item seem lower in cost, $19.99, for example), and bundle pricing (which is integrating multiple products and services into one overall package price).

demand. This is illustrated by our example changing the price from $5.00 to $6.00, which drives the attendance from 1000 to 800 (a 20% change in price has a 20% change in demand). Whatever service offered (e.g., attendance at an event, merchandise, instructional camps), it is indispensable to know the elasticity of the item, which, in turn, will show what flexibility one has in pricing it.

Pricing Objectives and Goals

Once a coach or program administrator has a picture of the price elasticity of the sports service, he or she will need to generate the pricing objectives and goals for that service. One should price the program's services to keep them in harmony with the program's overall goals. There are, in practice, "several pricing objectives that firms use. . . including pricing for survival, pricing to have a targeted return, pricing to increase market share, or pricing to maintain competitive position" (Luck and Ferrel, 1985). These objectives are straightforward and easily understandable. An objective fixed on survival is essentially an emergency approach to pricing that is designed to "keep the program afloat." The only consideration is to situate the price at whatever level makes it possible just to keep the business enterprise or program going. Pricing for a targeted return is principally determining a desired profit over and above the estimated costs and working the price to achieve the projected amount. Increasing market share and maintaining competitive position is basing the price on not only what the competition is doing but also on how one can aggressively establish and acquire more customers.

There is a technical method to the setting prices based on these objectives.

1. Find out how much control one has over price
2. Examine the costs to get a bottom price range
3. Examine customer attitude and behavior to set top price range and estimate price elasticity.
4. Set the strategic objectives to establish the final list price.
5. If necessary, discount the price to attract new customers using special offers. (Hiam, 1997)

Step 5 in the above pricing process is utilized when a program wants to stimulate sales in a condensed timeframe. In other words, discounting an established price is a short-term solution that can only be applied for limited periods. If it is discovered that the price level established is elastic at a certain level, the possibility of reevaluating the service price rather than repeatedly discounting should be examined.

Place/Distribution of Sports Services

The elementary difference between a tangible product and an intangible service (sport service) is most evident when discussing distribution. There are two ways to dispense sports services: either the customers come to the program's location or one must take the program's service to them. The key

Administrative Tip

Discounting can take on countless forms. Some primary methodologies are cash discounts, seasonal discounts, quantity discounts, and promotional discounts. Whichever technique one uses, remember that discounting is a short-term solution to stimulate sales and support. Its overuse can depreciate the worth and distinctiveness of a program.

to making a good choice between these two is accessibility. Ask which approach has the greatest potential to get the sports service to the largest number of customers. For example, if one's sport program is extremely visible, in a heavily populated area, and is easily accessible, the program's service distribution would undeniably have the customers come to the program. However, if the program is in a remote location with inadequate exposure, creative distribution might be required. The coach may need to take the sport service to an auxiliary locale to maximize customer interaction and sales.

Promotion of Sports Services

Promotion is the fourth and final component of the marketing mix.

> Promotion is communicating information between sellers and potential buyers to influence attitudes and behaviors. . . . [T]he main promotional job is to tell targeted customers that the right product is available, at the right price, at the right place (the first 3 Ps of the marketing mix). . . . [W]hat the marketer communicates is determined by customer needs and attitudes. . . . [H]ow the message is delivered depends on what blend of various promotional methods the marketing communicator chooses. (Perreault and McCarthy, 1996)

Promotion and advertising will be examined at length in the next chapter.

Customer Behavior and Satisfaction

The indispensable means to successfully implementing the program's marketing mix relates to the most important statement in business: *The customer is everything.* The number one priority should be to have this philosophy in mind no matter what the circumstance, activity, goal, or direction. Appreciating and satisfying the customer's needs and wants is vital in developing, maintaining, and increasing support.

Identifying how the consumer (in our case entertainment fan) makes his or her purchase determinations is crucial to understanding how to cultivate

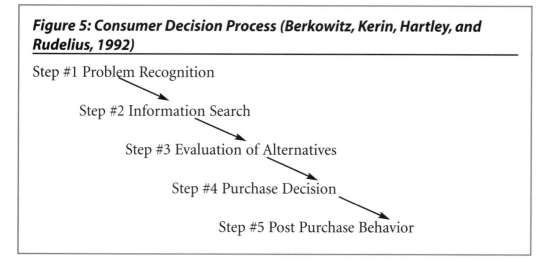

Figure 5: Consumer Decision Process (Berkowitz, Kerin, Hartley, and Rudelius, 1992)

Step #1 Problem Recognition

Step #2 Information Search

Step #3 Evaluation of Alternatives

Step #4 Purchase Decision

Step #5 Post Purchase Behavior

and retain customers. A substantial portion of practically every marketing text published today is dedicated to the fundamental, five-step consumer decision process (see Figure 5).

Every single purchase made by a consumer (no matter how large or small the purchase) goes through this five-step process. Sometimes the process can happen in literally a split second and in other cases it can take hours, days, or longer.

Step 1: Problem Recognition

We all have needs. They are the instinctual elements that provide each of us with the tools to survive, socialize, and achieve esteem. Abraham Maslow, in his historic, groundbreaking book, *Motivation and Personality,* contends that needs are hierarchal in nature and that the only way to attain higher, more luxurious desires is to make sure that our critical physiological and safety needs are satisfied first. The following is his graphic depiction of the hierarchy of needs (in ascending form).

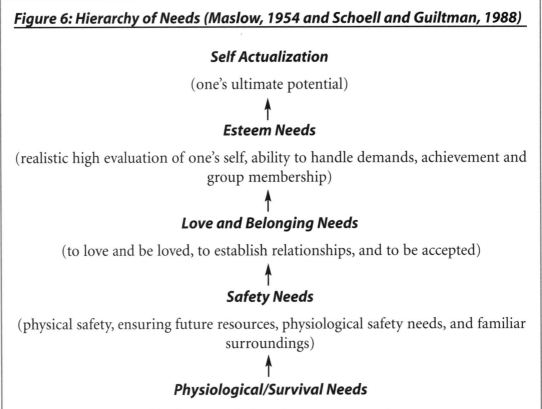

Figure 6: Hierarchy of Needs (Maslow, 1954 and Schoell and Guiltman, 1988)

Self Actualization

(one's ultimate potential)

↑

Esteem Needs

(realistic high evaluation of one's self, ability to handle demands, achievement and group membership)

↑

Love and Belonging Needs

(to love and be loved, to establish relationships, and to be accepted)

↑

Safety Needs

(physical safety, ensuring future resources, physiological safety needs, and familiar surroundings)

↑

Physiological/Survival Needs

(food, water, shelter, sleep, oxygen, etc.)

From a coaching perspective, discernment of human needs is the basis for identifying the program's target market and what the customers in that target market are looking for in a product or service. For example, an individual who is looking to satisfying the bottom level of needs in Maslow's Hierarchy model (physiological and safety) would not be concerned, at that point in time, with attending a sporting event. For target market identification, sports and entertainment focuses on groups who want to fulfill higher needs of belonging, esteem, and self-actualization. In the most direct terms, our product of sports entertainment is vying to meet the needs of people with disposable income over and above their survival and safety needs. The practical application of this theory narrows the market substantially.

Step 2: Information Search

Once people (or targeted groups) acknowledge a need that they must or would like to satisfy, they proceed to gather information about it.

> Information searches may be internal or external. Internal searching is a mental review of stored information relevant to the problem situation. This includes actual experiences, observations, and memories that could persuade marketing efforts. External searches is the gathering of information from outside sources. . . family members, friends, store displays, sales representatives, brochures, and other secondary sources. (Boone and Kurtz,1995)

The category of product or service will typically determine the extent to which individuals will seek out information for it. Products and services are typically classified as follows:

Convenience Products/Services: Little time and mental effort put into information search, low cost relative to customer base, everyday common purchases.

Shopping Products/Services: Moderate amount of time and mental effort exerted for information searching, substantial (but not consequential) cost, infrequent purchases.

Specialty Products/Services: Extensive amount of information search, big ticket and high cost purchases for customer base, very infrequent and rare purchases.

Our sports entertainment products and services need to be understood in terms of the type of product (convenience, shopping, or specialty) they represent to our customers. Each program has to verify its product classification as this will guide the marketing efforts and determine how much information the customer will demand.

For example, if a consumer is considering purchasing skybox tickets (or the entire box itself) for a professional sports season, he or she might consider that a specialty purchase. The professional team selling the tickets will furnish the customer with extensive information, focus its selling methods on a more personal level, and realize that since this is a specialty purchase and big cost item, they will need to furnish the consumer with the best options and services available. Conversely, if the ticket sales a consumer is considering are for a local high school sport, the purchase might be deemed more of a convenience purchase. For this type of sale, information will be supplied generally to a wide group (market), selling methods will be impersonal and open, and services will be limited.

Step 3: Alternative Evaluation

This is the point in the process that the consumers, after gathering all the significant information needed, look at all their choices. In other words, the

A coach or program administrator's job is to impart as much quality information as possible to current and potential supporters. The key is to find out the best and easiest avenues to convey the program information. This is done by understanding what means of information retrieval the program's supporters will use and then formatting information to fit these means.

consumer is comparing all of the possible alternatives that might satisfy his or her needs. "Consumer perceptions and values influence the evaluation of alternatives. . . advertising can seek to influence the criteria used to evaluate alternatives" (Kinnear, Bernhardt, and Krentler, 1995). The following model of the Consumer Decision-Making Framework contains the primary factors that influence consumers' perceptions and their alternative evaluations.

Figure 7 Consumer Decision-Making Framework (adapted from Schoell and Guiltinan, 1995)

Personality/Lifestyle
Our relative permanent tendency to behave in consistent ways in certain situations… they are consistent patterns that we follow in our lives.

Family
Many of our buying decisions are influenced by our upbringing. The brands we use as children often are the brands we perceive to be the best and continue to use later in life.

Learning
Influences on learning include
 Past experiences
 Brand loyalty
 Samples of new products
 Observing others
 Direct or indirect experience
 Frequency of promotional programs
 Talking with friends, sales people, family

Reference Groups
The groups that positively or negatively influence our attitudes and behaviors.

Consumer Decision Maker

Attitudes
The enduring feelings, evaluations, and response tendencies directed toward an object or idea.

Motivation
The driving force that causes a person to take ction to satisfy specific needs.

Social Class/Culture
The relatively stable divisions in society into which individuals, families, and groups share similar values, lifestyles, and behaviors. Additionally, our knowledge and cultural beliefs will determine our specific needs.

Perceptions
The process in which we choose relevant stimuli from the environment, organize them, and assign meaning to them.

These primary factors are what the program's advertising/promotional campaign should target. The desire is to have the consumer perceive that the program's product (athletic entertainment) is the finest option to fulfill their needs.

Step 4: Purchase Decision

"After choosing the best alternative, a person is ready for the purchasing act. . . the purchasing act includes deciding where to buy, agreeing to terms, and seeing if the items are available" (Evans and Berman, 1997). One straightforward directive is associated with the action of purchasing: Make it as simple and painless as possible. The worst thing that a program administrator can do is to make the purchase experience for the consumer complex and bewildering.

Step 5: Post-Purchase Behavior

The very last step in the decision-making process relates to the consumer's satisfaction with the service purchased, as this will influence how he or she will choose and behave the next time the same need surfaces. There is one noticeable phenomenon that takes place in this stage that one needs to attach importance to and concentrate on: cognitive dissonance or buyer remorse. Cognitive dissonance or buyer remorse

> is a state of anxiety brought on by the difficulty of choosing from among several alternatives. Unfortunately, for marketers, buyer remorse is common and if not addressed, the consumer may be unhappy with the chosen product even though it performs adequately. (Stanton, Etze, and Walker, 1994)

An outstanding way to minimize buyer remorse is to provide the customer with a quality product (in our instance a quality entertainment experience). The more costly the product, the more one needs to concentrate on cognitive dissonance. Followup contacts, personal notes, special promotions, and other related "perks" are all ways to ease buyer remorse.

Market Segmentation

Now that we have an underlying insight into the consumer decision-making process, the coach or program administrator should concentrate on the market, how to divide it up and, subsequently, which "piece of the pie" the program is going to target.

The formal definition of marketing segmentation is as follows:
> Segmentation is the process of partitioning markets into groups of potential customers with similar needs and/or characteristics who are likely to exhibit similar purchasing behavior. . . the objective of segmentation is to analyze markets, find niche opportunities, and capitalize on a superior competitive position. This is accomplished by selecting one (or more) group of users as targets for marketing activity and developing unique marketing programs to reach these prime prospects and market segments. (Weinstein, 1994)

Administrative Tip

When determining which target markets are appropriate for the program, do not dismiss any potential groups solely on the basis of opinion. Get concrete information. It is very possible that some of the program's most ardent supporters could be profiled groups that, on the surface, one would reject. For example, some senior citizen demographic groups could apparently be easily written off as potential supporters. Yet if secured as one of the program's target markets, they could be a powerful support and financial group.

From a coaching and program administration perspective, our inclusive market falls under the broad umbrella of entertainment. From there, we can narrow down our overall entertainment market to the smaller (but still substantial) sports entertainment market. The market of sports entertainment is the one we need to analyze, examine for niche opportunities, and approach in manner that capitalizes on our superior competitive position. Moreover, from the definition of marketing segmentation, we can determine that in order for us as coaches and program administrators to commit all of our existing resources to the correct target market segment we must

---

Figure 8: Market Segmentation (approximated from Harrel and Frazier, 1999)

Geographic
World Region
Economic Stage of Development
Nation
City Size and Density
Region
Climate
Zip Code

Demographic
Gender
Age
Income
Family Size
Family Life Cycle
Occupation
Education

Diversity
Religion
Race
Social Class

Psychographic
Life Style
Personality

Behavioristic
Readiness/Awareness
Ability and Experience
Loyalty
Shopping Habits
Usage

Benefits Sought
Delivery
Service
Price
Ease of Use

---

1. Categorize and segment the market into clear-cut, defined segments.
2. Select the most appropriate piece (or pieces) on which to focus our marketing mix—4 Ps.

In identifying segments, a marketer needs to research all of the possible bases for segmentation. One needs to investigate how the market is broken down into precise, identifiable groups. The potential ways to break down a market into distinct segments are described fully below.

Demographics are associated with population characteristics; geographic criteria relate to locations; psychographics are lifestyle choices; behavioral features are an individual and/or group's use of the product or service.

To get an all-inclusive and accurate market segmentation, each category and subcategory must be dissected for its relevance to the sports entertainment market. By questioning a market's demographics, geographics, and purchasing behavior, one is developing segmentation profiles of individuals and groups. For example, some categories might not have a significant effect on how a market is segmented. In sports entertainment, typically, city size and density are not applicable for sports fans who come from all diverse city sizes and densities.

The most useful application of this chart is for identifying the program's specific target market. With one's particular sport in mind, go through each category and develop a specific profile of the target market group.

1. Who are they? Go through the demographic and psychographics subcategories.
2. Where are they? Go through the geographic subcategories.
3. When will they buy? How will they buy? Why will they buy? Go through the behavioral subcategories.

   A few salient points on identifying target market segments:

   —Each sport, at each level of competition, will have its own distinctive segment (or, as our definition describes, niches).
   —Is it feasible to have more than one target market segment? Absolutely. One might come up with several target market segments in which the group profile is ideal for one's sport.
   —In evaluating and selecting the target market(s), "a firm must look at three factors: 1. segment size and growth, 2. segment structural attractiveness, and 3. the program's objectives and resources" (Kotler and Armstrong, 1997).

These three factors are described as follows:

1. Segment size and growth relate to sales, growth rate, and anticipated profitability of a segment.
2. Segment structural attractiveness defines the potency of the competition's ability to go after a given market segment. Availability or possibility of substitute products that can make customers switch affect a segment's attractiveness. The stronger each of these alternatives is, the less attractive the segment.
3. Program objectives and resources must always form the backdrop to determine if the segment is in line with the program's goals and

Administrative Tip

In selecting target markets, know the program's resource boundaries and limitations. For small athletic programs, a niche or focus strategy can bring a strong competitive advantage. If the target market niche is successfully captured by the program first, the program will be identified with that niche and be on the ground floor of future increased support. The key is finding a niche group that can sustain the program currently that also shows long-term growth potential.

whether the program possesses the capabilities, assets, and capital needed to take advantage of that segment.

If one can verify that the segment being evaluated is in an attractive group that presents an opportunity, that it has good profitability and growth potential, and is in line with the program's mission and resources, then it is an exemplary segment to pursue.

Summary

Marketing is the business function that facilitates exchanges in a corporate enterprise (in our case, athletic program). Externally, it helps coaches and program administrator to. . .

- Delineate outside environmental factors that influence a program.
- Analyze consumer behavior to their decision-making processes.
- Evaluate the overall market of sports entertainment and the segmentation of that market. In addition, segmentation will identify niche opportunities that give a program a defined target market in which to exert it efforts.

Internally, athletic program marketing. . .

- Examines product selection and development.
- Provides foundations for pricing a program's service.
- Elucidates the choices of distribution of a program's service.
- Communicates the benefits to potential consumers of the program's service.

The practical application of marketing by a coach/program administrator will escalate the program's exposure as well as increase revenues. It creates desires and action in program supporters and, if utilized correctly, it can transport a program to another operational level and competitive position.

Appendix 8A: Marketing Plan Outline

The conventional definition for a marketing plan:

> A document which formalizes a plan for marketing products and services. . . the plan has formal structure. . . and describes methods of applying marketing resources to achieve marketing objectives. (Westwood, 1998)

The marketing plan is a microdesign of the program's operational plan (Chapter 1). In other words, it is a "plan within a plan." Its mission, objectives, and strategies all emanate from the comprehensive program operational plan. It principally focuses on the marketing aspect of the program and how it will help accomplish the program's overall goals and mission.

The following is an outline of the marketing planning process. Note the close resemblance between marketing planning and organizational/program planning. Additionally, the concept of SWOT will be detailed in Chapter 13.

Figure 9: Market Planning Outline (adapted from Malcohm and Warren, 1997)

Phase One: Goals Setting

Step 1
Mission

Step 2
Corporate Objectives

Phase Two: Situational Review

Step 3
Marketing Audit

Step 4
Marketing SWOT Analysis

Step 5
Assumptions About Market and Marketing Situation

Phase Three: Strategy Formulation

Step 6
Marketing Objectives and Strategies

Step 7
Estimate Expected Results

Step 8
Identify Alternative Plans and Mixes

Phase Four: Resource Allocation and Monitoring

Step 9
Budgeting

Step 10
First Year Detailed Implementation Program
Measurement and Review

Chapter 9 ....

Athletic Program Promotion and Marketing Communication

Objectives

- To clarify the promotional communication concept and the promotional mix of advertising, direct marketing, sales promotion, personal selling, and public relations.
- To present the major strategic goals of marketing communication.
- To illustrate advertising avenues to coaches and program administrators.
- To familiarize coaches and program administrators with the advantages and disadvantages of the five major media outlets for advertising.
- To elucidate the promotional concept of AIDA.
- To present the advantages and disadvantages of direct marketing.
- To investigate sales promotion techniques.
- To acquaint coaches and program administrators with the personal selling process.

Introduction

The essential importance of Chapter 8, *Marketing Concepts*, cannot be stressed enough when discussing the role of promotion and communication. To blindly jump into advertising and promotion without consciously knowing the fundamentals of marketing would be at best a "hit or miss" proposition. These prerequisites provide focus to the program's marketing communication and promotion. Understanding market communication and promotion requires understanding of

- The marketing mix (product, pricing, distribution, and promotion) and how advertising is an interrelated component.
- How to distinguish and segment the market.
- How to choose a portion or segment to target the program's resources.
- How customers go through the purchasing process.
- How to construct a comprehensive marketing plan.

Promotional Tools

As previously clarified in Chapter 8, the fourth P in the marketing mix is promotion. Promotion is, in fact, marketing communication. Marketing communication consists of five major tools:

1. Advertising: Any paid form of nonpersonal presentation and promotion of ideas, goods, or services by an identifiable sponsor.
2. Direct Marketing: Use of mail, telephone, and other non-personal contact tools to communicate with or solicit a response from specific customers and prospects.
3. Sales Promotion: Short-term incentives to encourage purchase of a product or service.
4. Public Relations and Publicity: A variety of programs designed to promote and/or protect an organization's image of its individual products.
5. Personal Selling: Face-to-face interaction with one or more prospective customers for the purpose of making sales. (Bennett, 1988)

Marketing Communication Goals

Prior to discussing these five promotional and communication tools, a coach or program administrator will need to succinctly examine a series of some strategic goals pertaining to marketing communication:

1. Create Awareness: Inform markets about products, brands, stores, or organizations.
2. Build Positive Images: Build positive evaluations in peoples minds about the product, brand, store, or organization.
3. Identify Prospects: Find out names, addresses, and possible needs of potential buyers.
4. Build Relationships: Increase cooperation among stakeholders (internal and external).
5. Retain Customers: Create value for customers, satisfy their wants and needs, and earn their loyalty. (Churchill and Peter, 1998)

As a program administrator or coach, map out the program's objectives for a promotional communication campaign. Can one undertake and achieve multiple goals with a single campaign? Absolutely. In other words, can a coach put together a promotional communication strategy (by using advertising, direct marketing, sales promotions, public relations, and personal selling or a combination of these) that not only generates recognition for the program but also fosters positive perceptions and relationships while retaining and even increasing the program's customer bases? Yes. It is more complicated to have multiple goals, but if one is imaginative and can think the campaign through, there are no limits.

After conceiving and defining the goals for the program's promotion, examine the communication tools of advertising, direct marketing, sales promotion, public relations/publicity, and personal selling. Once again, it should be noted that a close examination of each of these tools is well beyond the scope of this book. In fact, each of these areas offers opportunity for study and is specialized career. Thus, it is not the purpose of this text to enable each reader to become an authority on these tools and their use. It is the purpose of this book to enable the reader to gain a working knowledge that will allow each of these tools to be adapted and utilized with purpose within the specific athletic program or team.

Administrative Tip

The vital key to any paid advertising campaign is reaching and then affecting the target market. Determine which advertising tools will have the most influence on the projected audience within budget constraints. Typically, quantity of messages communicated is not as important as quality of messages communicated. Think about which advertising tools will provide the program with the highest quality powerful message that will reach the target market efficiently.

Advertising

The prime promotional communication tool at a coach's or program administrator's disposal is advertising. Advertising is

> a form of impersonal, one-way mass communication paid for by the sponsor...it may be transmitted by many different media

---

Figure 1: Advertising Media

Media Advertising
Newspapers
Magazines
Trade Journals
Specialized Publications

Brochure Advertising
Media Guides
Game Day Programs
Specialized Literature

Broadcast Media
Television (local, regional, national)
Radio (local, regional, national)

Exhibitions
Special Events
Trade Show Displays

Internet
Web Pages
Banners

Video/Film
Promotional Videos and Films

Outdoor
Posters
Point-of-Purchase Displays
Billboards
Transit/Transportation Advertising
Signage Arena and Sports Facilities
Special Events
Aerial Advertising
Mobile Billboards
Movie Theatre Advertising

. . . examples include television, radio, newspapers, magazines, books, direct mail, and outdoor/billboards. (Lamb, Hair, and McDaniels, 1992)

From this list, the coach or program administrator can begin to uncover which advertising communication tool is desirable. In the 1998 text *Advertising and Promotion*, Michael and George Belch chart the advantages and disadvantages for each type of advertising/media communication tool (Figure 2).

Figure 2: Media Advantages and Disadvantages (Belch and Belch, 1998)

Media	Advantages	Disadvantages
Television	Mass Coverage High Reach Impact of Sight and Sound Low Cost Per Exposure Attention Getting Favorable Image	Low Selectivity Short Message Life High Absolute Cost High Production Costs Clutter
Radio	Local Coverage Low Cost High Frequency Flexible Low Production Costs Well Segmented Audience	Audio Only Clutter Low Attention Getting Fleeting Message
Magazines	Segmentation Potential Quality Reproduction High Information Content Longevity Multiple Readers	Long Lead Time Visual Only Lack of Flexibility
Newspapers	High Coverage Low Cost Short Lead Time Selective Ad Placement Timely Reader Controls Exposure Coupons	Short Life Clutter Low Attention Getting Poor Reproduction Quality Selective Reader Impact
Outdoor	Location Specific High Repetition Easily Noticed	Short Exposure Time Poor Image Location Restrictions

After researching each type of advertising communication tool for its germane advantages and disadvantages, the ultimate criteria for selecting an advertising mix (which is a package of tools to promote the athletic program) is financial. The advertising goal from a financial standpoint is simple and uncomplicated. Which advertising tool (or tools) should the program employ to amplify its target market exposure and get the most from its limited advertising dollars? This is where the previously discussed subject of program marketing comes into play and affects advertising communication. Knowing the customers (and prospective customers) is the salient key. Through market segmentation and subsequent target market selection, a program administrator or coach can get a well-defined profile of current and potential supporters. This segment profile will furnish answers to questions such as the following:

- Who are they?
- Where are they?
- What type of people are they?
- What are their demographics? Psychographics? Geographics? Lifestyles?
- When is the best time to communicate with them?
- How often do they need promotional communication?

With these customer profile questions answered (through marketing planning), the question of how to contact and persuade the customer becomes easier. In the simplest terms, one must know the current and potential customers before one can promote and communicate with them. After determining who the customer is, match the financial resources up with the most effective advertising tools the program can afford. Hopefully the program's financial budget will support those tools.

Once the program is connected with its potential customers, the concept of creativity comes into play. Marketing communication should follow the AIDA concept. The acronym is explained below.

Attention: The advertising tools utilized must first secure the customer's attention. In a majority of all advertising, one has a precious few seconds to achieve this. Since we are all saturated with a continued bombardment of advertising, if one does not "catch and grab" the prospective customer's *attention* instantaneously, he or she will move on.

Interest: After successfully getting customers' attention, the advertising communication must seize their *interest*. In other words, once they are *grabbed* they must be *held* until the message is delivered.

Desire: Subsequent to getting prospective customers' attention and interest, one must get them to *desire* the program's product (or in our case, entertainment service.). If the advertising is imaginative and directed toward the program's target market, developing the desire for the service is the next progressive step in the AIDA progression.

Action: This is the final stage. If A, I, and D are fulfilled, getting the customer to purchase and to support the program should fall in line.

In today's world, the concept of creativity in advertising is crucial. If one wants to achieve AIDA, the creative advertising work must be focused on what the customers are interested in. Appendix 9A covers two different, step-by-step procedures for creating attention-grabbing promotional communications. While these two procedures provide structure for the creative process, the actual inspiration and generation of ideas typically comes from

Administrative Tip

Because advertising is using the most important organizational resource—money—conduct extensive research to provide a distinct supporter profile. Quantify as much of the program's research as possible. Knowing the supporters is the first step in reaching them.

Administrative Tip

AIDA takes creativity. Creativity can be an intrinsic trait or it can be inspired by others. It is possible not to have creativity as part of one's personal make-up. If this is the case, then recruit people with the gift of creativity. As a coach or program administrator, a well-defined strength can be recognizing and accepting one's own weaknesses.

nonstructured techniques such as brainstorming and free association methods.

Direct Marketing

Direct marketing is defined as "a direct form of communication with customers. . . direct communication is a one-on-one dialog through computers, the mail, video and touch tone phones" (Well, Burnett, and Moriarty, 1992). The key to contacting large volumes of individual prospects though direct marketing techniques comes from advances in technology and is known in business as mass customization. Mass customization enables mass-produced products (or in this case, advertising and promotion) to be customized for each individual.

Administrative Tip

A conspicuous danger in direct mailing is saturation. Temper and monitor the number of direct contacts the program has with its supporters. If the program exceeds tolerable direct contacts with its support groups, not only will the messages be disregarded, but they might instill a negative perception of the program in the eyes of the supporters.

Another important aspect of direct marketing is the development of a substantial database of qualified target market customers. The operative word in the last sentence is *qualified*. A phone book is a viable database of potential customers. For our programs, would a phone book be a qualified database?

More than likely, it would not. How does one find a suitable database to use for direct marketing purposes? Such a database should come from the market segmentation process discussed in Chapter 8.

To review:
1. Identify the program's overall operational market.
2. Break down the market into segments of people with similar needs, wants, characteristics, and purchasing behavior.
3. Select the most appropriate segment on which to focus organizational efforts.
4. Profile the selected segment to find the most efficient way to contact prospects through one of the aforementioned direct marketing techniques.

As mentioned, direct marketing techniques are managed through databases. There are two ways to gain access to a database. The first and more difficult way is to construct one's own. To do so, find potential supporters, design the system of data retrieval and use, and then catalog and computerize the list. The second option is to utilize a database that already exists. The sources of databases that already exist are plentiful, and through the ever-growing power of computers, the number of relevant lists available is continuously increasing. Whether it is a geographic, demographic, psychographic, or behavioral database, never forget that the program's segment profile will determine which one (or ones) to utilize.

As with all forms of communication, direct marketing involves extensive planning and research as well as creativity tactics, cohesion of concepts, target market appeal, AIDA, and production and distribution systems. Whatever direct marketing techniques are selected to reach the target market segment, one must know the advantages and disadvantages of each technique. The following is an advantage and disadvantage table of direct marketing.

> **Figure 3: Advantages and Disadvantages of Direct Marketing (adapted from Belch and Belch, 1998)**
>
> ### Advantages
>
> **Selective Reach:** Direct marketing can reach a large number of people and reduces waste coverage. Consumers with the highest potential are covered.
>
> **Segmentation Capabilities:** Database listings allow marketers to segment on the basis of geographic area, occupation, demographics, and job title, to mention just a few variables.
>
> **Frequency:** With a concentrated target market listing, direct marketing may not need the same frequency of use as other advertising and promotional communication.
>
> **Flexibility:** Direct marketing can take on a variety of creative forms.
>
> **Timing:** Direct response advertising can be much more timely…it can be put together very quickly and distributed to a target market.
>
> **Personalization:** No other advertising media can personalize a message as well as direct marketing.
>
> **Costs:** Direct marketing may be high on an absolute basis but because of focused targeting, its ability to specifically target the audience and eliminate waste can reduce costs.
>
> **Measures of Effectiveness:** Feedback from direct marketing is immediate and always accurate.
>
> ### Disadvantages
>
> **Image Factor:** Direct marketing has a historical image of being "junk mail."
>
> **Accuracy:** The effectiveness of all of the advantages to direct marketing is a function of how accurate the database lists are. Inaccurate lists minimize effectiveness.
>
> **Content Support:** It is difficult in direct marketing to create a mood due to the limits of the media.
>
> **Computerization Limits:** Computers have not been adopted at the rate expected. Many people prefer their news and promotional communication in a more typical medium such as television or radio rather than computers.

It would serve a coach or program administrator well to do a cost-benefit analysis (based on the above advantages and disadvantages) to evaluate whether direct marketing is warranted and financially feasible. The investment of time and money in putting together a direct marketing plan is extensive. Once again, the ultimate determinant of whether to utilize any promotional tools is the customer. Through analysis, if direct marketing is proven to be effective and the financial resources of the program can support a direct marketing campaign, then it is a powerful and focused promotional instrument.

Sales Promotion

Sales promotion is defined as "those marketing activities, other than personal selling, advertising, and publicity, that stimulate consumer purchasing. . . they are various nonrecurring selling efforts not in the ordinary routine" (AMA, 1960). These nonrecurring techniques are used to create awareness and to stimulate sales. Some of the possible sales promotion techniques include rebates, coupons, samples, etc. From a sports administrative perspective, the creativity that goes into sales promotion techniques can be rich and rewarding.

The following chart lists sales promotion techniques along with their relative cost and time considerations.

Figure 4: Sales Promotional Techniques (Hingston, 2001)

Comparing Different Promotional Ideas

Promotion	Relative Cost	Relative Time
Business Lunches	Low	Low
Competitions/Raffles	Highly Variable	Low to Medium
Coupons/Gift Certificates/		
Loyalty Cards	Highly Variable	Medium to High
Fashion Shows	Medium	Medium
Free Gifts	Highly Variable	Low
Free Trials	Low	Low
In-Store Demos	Low	Low to Medium
Joint Ventures	Highly Variable	Medium
Mail Shots	Low to Medium	Medium
Newsletters	Medium to High	High
Samples	Low	Low
Open Houses	Medium	Medium
Videos and CDs	Medium to High	High

Once again, it must be emphasized that while relative cost and time are important considerations in choosing a sales promotion, the most critical choice factor is the program's target market and the market's receptivity to a certain sale promotion technique. No matter how time- and cost-effective a sales promotional method could be, if it does not stimulate or support sales, it is inappropriate and will squander program resources.

Personal Selling

Personal selling is one-on-one, face-to-face interaction between a coach or program administrator (or program representative) and a prospective supporter. The benefits of a successful sales call can be immeasurable. Not only can a personal sales call close an immediate sale, it also establishes a personal rapport for future encounters. This, in turn, can lead to "positive word of mouth" networking that creates more sales. Virtually every marketing and advertising text goes through a step-by-step procedure to make a sales presentation (or to close a personal sale). While there are slight variations in the stages, content, and sequencing, each sales person, to be successful, has to have "some common sales qualities. A successful sales person is persuasive, more intuitive than analytical, outgoing, motivated by prestige and power, possesses a high level of energy, is dominant but not domineering, is empathic, and driven by a high ego" (Hisrich, 1990).

The following is one of the many step-by-step procedures that can be used in making a sales presentation and closing a sale.

Figure 5: Personal Sales Presentation (Kotler and Armstrong, 1993)

Step 1   Prospecting and Qualifying
Identifying qualified potential customers

Step 2   Preapproach
Learn as much about prospective client before making sales call

Step 3   Approach
Meeting the potential customer to start a relationship

Step 4   Presentation/Demonstration
Tell the story of the product and/or service

Step 5   Handle Objections
Seek out, clarify, and overcome objections of potential customers

Step 6   Closing
Ask for order

Step 7   Followup
After sales activity to ensure customer satisfaction and repeat business

---

Personal selling goes beyond a generic communication tool. Personal selling has been referred to as a business skill or science that takes hard work and extensive experience to master. It is composed of. . . .

- Building relationships, both short term and long term.
- Providing adept demonstrations.
- Interpersonal recommendations.
- Showmanship and presentation dynamics.
- Tactical negotiation.
- Networking and campaigning.
- Role playing and performing for affect.

For a coach or program administrator to exploit this methodology in program promotion and communication, one must set aside the time to appreciate and understand the process as well as to rehearse and practice its use.

Administrative Tip

AIDA is pertinent with all communication tools, especially sales promotions. Sales promotions, to be valuable, must concentrate totally on the support group and its tendencies. If one truly knows who the program supporters are, think through what sales promotion techniques will grab their attention and get them to take action.

Summary

Marketing communication encompasses four primary promotional elements: advertising, direct marketing, sales promotion, personal selling, and public relations (Chapter 10). The promotional mix of these devices is through a planned process that takes into account goals, budgets, and, ultimately, the program's target market. The effectual combination of these tools can maximize a program's exposure, image, and support. However, it should be reiterated that marketing communication is a part of the whole concept of marketing. By itself and without the proper background concepts of the marketing mix, it will inescapably fail to achieve it intentions.

APPENDIX 9A: Creative Strategy Outline/Blueprinting

SECTION 1: Creative Strategy Outline (Hart, 1998)

The 4D approach to creating an effective ad stands for the 4 Dimensions of Creativity. The breakdown is as follows:

First Dimension

Pinpoint the single selling idea. . . the particular consumer need that the brand satisfies.
- Understand the consumer's needs and attitudes.
- Appreciate what competitive brands are offering.
- Select and define what our brand will offer and to whom.

Second Dimension

Create the most effective and appealing expression of the idea.
- Recognize the real problem of getting the consumer's attention and what is already competing for it.
- Make sure the selling message is clear, distinctive, believable, and convincing in consumer terms.
- Create in all material an equally clear, distinctive total identity and underline the brand name.

Third Dimension

Find the most effective media to communicate the idea.
- Select the media that reach the right people.
- Choose the media best capable of carrying the message.
- Use the media with the greatest impact and economy.

Fourth Dimension

Eliminate uncertainty as far as possible before and after the advertising appears.
- See whether research can help.
- Be creative and forward looking in the use of research.
- Present results clearly to help decision making.

A methodological approach such as this does not replace creativity. It merely channels the creative process through each stage of development in a minimum amount of time and with the maximum effect.

SECTION 2: Creative Blueprinting (Keding and Bivins, 1990)

People in advertising speak of creative blueprinting in the same way an architect may speak of a house plan. Creative blueprinting gives each advertising assignment and campaign structure and form.

The following is a list of components in a creative blueprint:
- Product Description: What the product or service offers and how the supporter and consumer may use it.
- Target Audience: A summary of relevant audience.

- Competition: Who the direct and indirect competition is.
- Problem Advertising Is to Solve: Identification of the communication problems to be solved by advertising.
- Advertising Objective: A clear statement declaring what the advertising will accomplish.
- Features and Benefits: A summary of the products and services benefits. . . rank them in order of importance. The most important will be the center of the advertising.
- Positioning: A statement claiming a place for the product or service in the minds of the target audience.
- Tone and Manner : The feeling the advertising will convey.
- Premise and Blueprint Statement: A sentence or two that synthesizes all of the above information.

The points are in no particular order. The key is for the coach to become familiar with the process to come up with and then develop ideas that generate superior advertising.

Chapter 10 ....

Public Relations in Sports Programs

Objectives

- To introduce and describe the concept of public relations.
- To explain the distinction between a public relations campaign and perpetual public relations.
- To examine the stages in a public relations campaign.
- To assess perpetual public relations systems.
- To illuminate tactics in handling a public relations crisis.

Introduction

As coaches and program administrators, we have the capacity to be the most significant individuals in how the public perceives and identifies our program, sport, and industry. Coaches can develop cooperative relationships with prominent individuals, groups, and the overall community through the deployment of publicity and public relation systems. These collective relationships foster program goodwill, an optimistic perception of the program, and receptive communication channels between internal and external stakeholders. While the development of these relationships may seem unsystematic and governed by informal styles, the concept of public relations and publicity is conceived, developed, and implemented through tangible, coordinated procedures.

While the creation of a positive image is an important goal of publicity and public relations, it must be emphasized that PR's primary intention is to be a part of the program's inclusive marketing concept (Chapters 8 and 9). Marketing communication techniques such as advertising, direct marketing, sales promotion, and personal selling are all applied in harmony with public relations. In the simplest terms, public relations, as a marketing tool, directly and indirectly helps facilitate sales and exchanges.

Public Relations Defined

From an academic standpoint, public relations has numerous definitions that vary in substance and structure. For our purpose, the following description encompasses the fundamental nature of publicity and public relations for sports programs.

> Publicity is the principal tool used in the wooing and winning public opinion to achieve good public relations. . . a good public image, established through positive publicity, shows up on the profit side of the ledger. . . publicity tells the story an organization wants the public to know. It is the face the organization presents, through media, to the public. (Smith, 1991)

A core consideration that this analysis underscores is the need to develop and preserve a highly regarded public image. This corporate identity (or in our case, program identity) is the context not only for the way people think of the program now, but also for the way they imagine the program in the future. If the program's impression is one that elicits upbeat, positive feelings, the program's public relations foundation is sound and can be built on. If the current program image has little or no response (neither positive nor negative) associated with it, one can look at this situation from a "clean slate" viewpoint and the program's public relations outlook is an opportunity for growth. Finally, and regrettably, if the program's image provokes negative connotations, one will need to stem the tide of disapproving opinion and start the lengthy process of building an optimistic picture for the program.

As with most business applications, public relations and publicity need a formal proactive plan. For athletic programs it should be clarified that public relations has two distinct elements. The first is known as *campaign public relations* and the second is *perpetual public relations*. The difference between the two is captured by the factors of frequency and duration. Public relations campaigns are one-time projects with a fixed, terminal timeframe. Perpetual public relations is a continual process set up (through a public relations system) to operate as long as a program is functioning. Campaigns are associated with intensive development efforts and attempts to reach identified goals, while perpetual public relations systems are characterized by long-term maintenance and consistency.

Public Relations Campaigns

Figure 1 below identifies the stages in a public relations campaign.

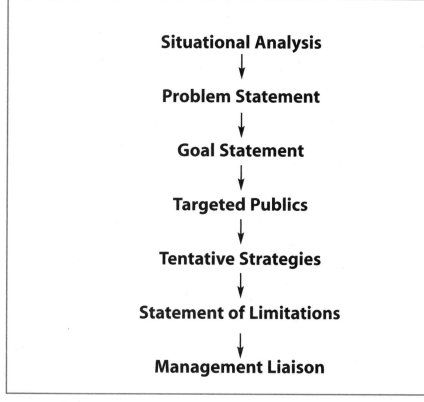

Figure 1: Public Relations Campaign Stages (Kendall, 1996)

Situational Analysis
↓
Problem Statement
↓
Goal Statement
↓
Targeted Publics
↓
Tentative Strategies
↓
Statement of Limitations
↓
Management Liaison

Administrative Tip

Two prevalent usages of the word *campaign* in our society are when speaking of political battles and military operations. Think of the program's public relations campaign as a political and military crusades with one's position as the coach or program administrator being the equivalent of a politician or military commander. The program's campaign will undoubtedly use military or political tactics to attain its objectives.

Situational Analysis

The initiating phase in a public relations campaign, situational analysis, is known as a "where are we now" perspective:

> [sometimes] called a communication audit, the purpose of the analysis is to uncover the contemporary image of the program and to delineate the state of hostility, prejudice, apathy, or ignorance [that it engenders]. It is no use planning a campaign unless one knows where the program is now. (Jefkins, 1993)

Additionally, during this current-time analysis, conduct a preliminary public relations SWOT investigation. To be discussed later in Chapter 13 of this text, SWOT analysis involves a thorough evaluation of the program's internal strengths and weaknesses along with its external opportunities and threats. A SWOT study is appropriate for all business functions within a program and, as we shall see, especially public relations.

Administrative Tip

As with all introspective program investigations, the public relations situational analysis must be as unemotional and as dispassionate as possible. A truthful assessment is the key to a thriving campaign.

Problem Statement

While the phrase *problem statement* has a pessimistic connotation, it does not have to be negative in context. With the help of a SWOT analysis, the coach or program administrator may have discovered encouraging opportunities and notable strengths. The problem statement should be as clear-cut and concise as possible. Clarity is essential since the public rela-

Administrative Tip

Dig deep to expose the program's true public relations problem, not just its symptoms. Even though the symptoms might initially seem like they are the bona fide predicament, they are more than likely superficial signs of something more profound.

tions campaign, whatever it is designed to achieve, will emanate from this declaration.

Goal Statement

Administrative Tip

Since public relations campaigns have precise time frames, their goals should be very time specific while focusing directly on the validated public relations problem. In other words, can the campaign's goals be accomplished within its operational deadlines.

A goal statement

> should be evaluated by asking (1) does it really address the situation? (2) is it realistic and achievable? and (3) can success be measured in meaningful terms? Public relations basically have two kinds of goals: informational and motivational. Informational objectives are goals designed primarily to expose audiences to information and create awareness. . . the difficulty with an informational objective is in measuring how well the objective has been achieved. . . motivational objectives try to change attitudes and influence behavior. . . because they are bottom-line oriented, they are based on measurable results that can be clearly quantified. (Wilcox, Ault, and Agee, 1998)

From a sports program viewpoint, an informational public relations goal could be to provide a website for fans and supporters to access data about the program's players and staff. A motivational public relations objective could be to inform and energize the target market (through various media) about an upcoming event. The quantifiable measurement to see if this goal was accomplished could simply be by tickets sold and/or stands filled. Once again, it is essential to understand that whatever type of objective one chooses, the objective should be in line with the program's public relations problem statement, which is directly aligned with the marketing mission statement, which, in turn, closely reflects the program's mission statement.

Targeted Publics

The idea of *targeted public relations segments* corresponds with the marketing concept of *target markets*. In other words, one should find the targeted public relations groups the same way that one established (and exploited) the target market group(s). Look at the public as a whole, segment it into groups with similar wants, needs, characteristics, and perceptions, then select the target groups on which the program will concentrate its available resources. Will the public relations target group be the same as the marketing target group? Possibly, perhaps even likely, but not always. It depends on the goals, the situation, and what one is attempting to achieve. From a bottom-line approach, motivational goals will produce very comparable public relations and marketing targets. Inspirational goals might be broader in nature because they are trying to create awareness in a larger population.

Tentative Strategies

Tentative strategies in the planning process are exactly that: preliminary strategies to achieve the program's public relations goals. From targeting, the coach or program administrator knows whom he or she is going to attempt to reach. This stage answers questions like the following:

- How am I going to reach them?
- What type of media would best get their attention?
- What message do I develop? What story do I want told?
- What type of creativity should I employ?
- How frequently do the targeted groups need to be exposed to the message?
- When should I reach them?
- Is my message ethical? Legal? Factual?
- If they get our message, when should we see results?
- Ultimately, will the strategy work?

As one goes through the inventory of strategic questions, each specific tactic will have its own distinct set of issues. The more thoroughly these types of questions are asked, the higher the likelihood that the chosen tactic will work and the public relations goal will be realized.

Statement of Limitation

The statement of limitation is principally the "W" (weaknesses internally in the program) of the SWOT investigation. In other words: What internal deficiencies (lack of skills and/or resources) does the program have that might affect its projected public relations strategies and goals? Skills can relate to managerial abilities, knowledge base, and technical know-how, among others. Resources directly relate to personnel, time resources, and, ultimately, financial constraints.

Management Liaison

The concluding step in the public relations campaign process, management liaison, might not pertain to all sports programs. If the program is considered autonomous and thus functions without peripheral, external influences, the managerial liaison phase is not applicable. However, if the program operates as one unit within a larger department or if it has a controlling board, owner, or committee, then, as the program administrator, one must act as the managerial liaison. The managing group will need to (in some cases) authorize the program's public relations plan, sanction it through funding, provide their input and insight, etc. Each situation and program will have different reporting criteria.

Perpetual Public Relations

Perpetual public relations is how, on a permanent and continuous basis, a coach or program administrator enlightens, informs, and communicates with the media and the public. Public relations relates to the business concepts of operating systems, policies, and procedures. The public relations system, in which the program communicates externally, is the way staff members interact and who is specifically responsible for them. Public relations policies and procedures within established systems are more specific rules and step-by-step 'how to's'.

Before developing and implementing a perpetual public relations system, it is crucial that one both define what a system is and delineate its

Administrative Tip

When considering the statement of limitations, inventory the internal weaknesses (in priority order) that might impair the campaign, and then set down achievable solutions to combat those weaknesses. Evaluate the prospective outcomes from a resources viewpoint: time, money, and manpower being the primary considerations. In other words, distinguish which weaknesses must be addressed for the campaign to be successful, prioritize their solutions, and outline the resources to be allocated to them.

Administrative Tip

In the capacity of managerial liaison, a coach or program administrator must understand that to be successful, he or she must maintain open lines of communication with all relevant program stakeholders. Keeping everyone continually informed throughout all aspects of the campaign is essential. Conversely, one needs to balance the amount of information given so as not to inundate people with trivial information.

components. While the system concept in the 1994 text, *Introduction to Information Systems* is geared toward technological and computer applications in organizations, the author does provide the structural definition and essential ingredients to describe any system. The following is an abridged explanation of the system concept and its functions:

> A system can be simply defined as a group of interrelated or interacting elements forming a unified whole. . . a system is a group of interrelated components working together toward a common goal by accepting inputs and producing outputs in an organized transformation process. . . a dynamic system has three basic interacting function/parts: Inputs involve capturing and assembling elements that enter the system to be processed. Processing involves the transformation processes that convert inputs to outputs. Outputs involve transferring elements that have been produced by the transformation process to their ultimate destination. (O'Brien, 1994)

From this uncomplicated description of systems, one can develop a program's public relations system and procedures. Ask the following supporting questions to systemize the program's public relations. These questions are nonspecific and in no particular order. The organization's operating environment will dictate the precise questions.

Inputs/Resources

- What type of equipment will the program need to have for a professional, proficient public relations communication system?
- What type of human resource needs will the public relations system demand?
- What are the individual qualifications and expertise that will be needed on the program's public relations staff?
- What type of printing service is available? Postal services? Email and database availability?
- What access does the program have to internal organizational staff who could be utilized for speaking engagements and interviews?
- For athletic programs that rely on statistics, what type of statistical tracking software is considered necessary?

Processing: Converting Inputs to Outputs

- Who is accountable for. . .
  —press releases
  —compiling statistics
  —assembling press kits
  —securing interviews
  —speaking engagements
  —public relations events
- What are the step-by-step actions for constructing the above public relations items?

- Who is responsible for scheduling, organizing, and operating public relations functions?
- Are the program's conversion processing activities computerized? If so, are these procedures the most up-to-date for efficiency?

Outputs/Final Product

- Is the final public relations product professional?
- Is it factual and accurate?
- Is it relevant to readers/listeners?
- Does it "tell the story" that one would like?
- Is it reaching the media in an opportune, timely manner?
- Is the produced output targeted toward appropriate sources?

Two other components that are of great consequence to a high-quality public relations system are feedback and control. Questions that will refine the program's public relations system that deal with these two components are as follows:

Feedback/Reverse Communication

- What was the external reaction to and opinion regarding the public relations communication?
- Is the program getting the public relations exposure expected?
- Is the public relations output the same as the public relations media coverage given?

Control/Adjustments to the System

- Is the program attaining its public relations goals?
- If not, how can the coach or program administrator modify the program's inputs, processes, and outputs to improve results?

To reiterate, the key to putting together a well-designed public relations systems is to establish successful procedures and to monitor the overall process.

Crisis Public Relations

No matter what business or sports program one operates, the subject of crisis public relations is not only important but, sadly, is a fact of life. Accidents can happen at any moment. People make unforeseen mistakes. Program communications can be misconstrued from their original intention. How one handles events and public relations "nightmares" could determine the program's survival or the course of one's career. Is it better to have a plan for potential problems? Absolutely.

> No organization can plan for every contingency. . . the what now model details procedures to be followed in whatever emergency may befall. The points to consider when a crisis strikes:
> - Accept that it is a problem.
> - Gather the facts.
> - Throw all available resources into the problem.

Administrative Tip

Perpetual public relations systems require time to cultivate key media relationships and feedback. As the program's visible leader, spend time developing positive relations with key media personnel. Goodwill and trust are earned so be patient and persistent.

- Maintain an open flow of information once the story is known.
- Establish a pattern of disclosure about the issue.
- Alert corporate communications immediately.
- Establish emergency alert procedure.
- Establish a centralized spokesperson.
- Establish a press corps station.
- Track questions received.
- Don't release information prematurely.
- Don't speculate.
- Correct false information.
- Keep information flowing.
- Continue to ask "what's next" and plan followup coverage. (Dilenschneider and Forrestal, 1987)

Some important lessons can be derived from the above 14 points. First and foremost, never take a "defensive stance" in a public relations emergency. This posture will only provoke an aggressive response from supporters and media. Additionally, once the program (and coach or program administrator) adopts an it's-not-our-fault mindset, it is virtually impossible to turn around and reverse that position. Another lesson that can be derived from the 14 points is *to think*. In other words, think through all aspects first (think before speaking). Comments made off the cuff and without proper judgment can actually compound and, in some cases, accentuate the crisis. Lying to curtail problems will, in fact, exponentially increase the crisis as soon as the lie is discovered (and lies almost always will be exposed). Finally, it is necessary to have good communication both internally and externally throughout the crisis. The choice of the right spokesperson is imperative. Spokespersons must be able to monitor and curtail their emotions, communicate the story that the program wants told, and only answer questions for which the answers are substantiated. Their most central characteristic should be that they do not get rattled and are unflappable under pressure. A display of panic can discredit the speaker and the message being communicated.

Summary

The potential for the use of public relations campaigns for sports programs is considerable. The most salient point is that the expenditures associated with public relations are, in comparison to other promotional and marketing communication techniques, minimal. For sports programs with nominal funding, PR can be a compelling, cost-effective tool. Another significant aspect of public relations is it is perceived by the public as more credible and convincing in comparison with paid promotional approaches. Other promotional techniques, such as advertising, are seen as manipulative, while public relations articles and editorials are taken as more factual and genuine. Finally, public relations is proactive in nature. If continually used, even when the program is encountering little or no public instability and disapproving opinion, it can "build up positive points" for the time when there is a crisis situation involving the program. If a publicity predicament never occurs (which is doubtful in any organization), then the constructive benefits still remain.

APPENDIX 10A: News Releases

The following section provides sports administrators and coaches with a fundamental format for copy presentation for program news releases. The outline is extrapolated from *The Publicity Kit: A Complete Guide for Entrepreneurs, Small Businesses and Non-Profits* (Smith, 1991).

Professional Appearance

1. Appearance Guidelines
   —Neatness counts. . . no typos, misspellings, or cross-outs.
   —Do not use exotic typefaces. . . scripts and italics are harder to read.
   —Use business size, 8 1/2" by 11" paper. . . do not use onion skin, colored, or erasable paper.
   —Keep handy a current directory of the program's list of officers, managers, directors, and employees.
2. Tools of the Trade
For quick reference:
   - A good dictionary close for spelling and meanings.
   - A thesaurus to identify synonyms for frequently used words.
   - *The UPI Stylebook* and *Associated Press Stylebook and Libel Manual*.
   - *The Elements of Style*.

Preparation of News-Release Copy

1. Format Guidelines
   - Type release on the organization's letterhead. If there is no such official letterhead, create one for the program.
   - Use white bond paper. Display the organization's logo, address, email, fax, and phone number.
   - Type on only one side of the paper.
   - Leave ample margins (1 1/2" all around).
   - Give each newspaper in the same geographic area a release with a different lead. . . provide a local angle in the lead.
   - Never end the page so that a part of a sentence or a single word ends up on the next page. If possible, do not end a page in the middle of the paragraph.
   - Write concisely, in a simple-to-understand style.
   - If sending copies, have a good, clear, sharp original copy. If at all possible, have it copied professionally.
   - Use paperclips to fasten pages together. Do not staple.
   - Be sure to keep a dated copy in the program's file.
2. Format Instructions
Letterhead document always with
   Name
   Address
   Telephone Number
   Email
   Fax

Type contact information immediately below the letterhead. Align contact information at the left margin and align each phone number under each name.

Contact section should contain the following:

- The word "Contact" then contact's name.
- Telephone Number.
- "Alternate Contact" name and telephone number below primary name.
- Two lines under contact section, insert (flush left) a "Summary Headline." Type headline in upper/lower case.
- Type release timing line.
- For Immediate Release.
- Release at Your Convenience.
- For Release on (Specific Date).
- Indicate if the story is an exclusive. Type "EXCLUSIVE" in capital letters above release time line.
- Type mailing date.
- Insert a dateline. A dateline is the city and state from which the story originates.
- Indicate if the story runs more than one page. Type at bottom center.
- On each succeeding page, type a line using a shortened version of the summary headline. Follow that with a page number.
- Signify the end of the release by typing (at end of print).

Copy Preparation Tips

- Never trust the typist.
- Proofread each page.
- Never play favorites among newspaper editors and columnists.
- Never double plant. Double planting means submitting the same story to more than one person at the same publication.
- Check that all names are proper given names.
- Dates should be displayed as day first, month next, year last.
- Check and recheck spelling of names.
- Look up the meaning and spelling of words.
- If a note is included, attach it with a paperclip.
- Remember KISS: Keep it short, simple.
- Better never than late. . . give publications at least 24 hours prior to the day of publication. For events, submit them one or two weeks in advance.

Section IV ....

External Program Administration and Other Business Applications

Section IV External Program Administration and Other Business Applications

Section four of the book discusses external environmental business elements and how they interact with sports program administration.

- Chapter 11 not only looks into distinctive types of fundraising activities but also investigates fundraising program structure. Each fundraising endeavor is broken down into annual or capital fundraising. The activities are also scrutinized as to their rationale, make-up, and components.
- Chapter 12 identifies an increasingly important subject in sports administration and coaching: program risk management. The four major areas of athletic program risk management are described in addition to insurance criteria and selection of insurance coverage.
- Chapter 13 covers the groundbreaking, advanced theories of strategic management as they relate to sports administration and coaching. The underlying objective of this chapter is to provide coaches and program administrators with significant, established models of strategic management as they relate to positioning, operational tactics, and environmental analysis.
- Chapter 14 discusses the models of business ethics and how those models can be employed or adapted to the world of coaching or program administration. The practicalities of ethical decision making and the evaluation of each individual's ethical decision-making process are emphasized

Chapter 11 ....

Program Fundraising

Objectives

- To characterize program fundraising and clarify the three major areas of fundraising for athletic programs.
- To distinguish the underlying difference between annual and capital fundraising.
- To offer and explain 10 possible program fundraising activities.
- To present the essential groundwork for additional program fundraising activities.

Introduction

This chapter imparts concrete techniques for the athletic program function of fundraising. The importance of fundraising is determined by the financial position of the organization. If the existing monetary status of the program warrants fundraising, the athletic program's uses for the augmented contributions, gifts, and donations can be unlimited. Fundraising can supplement salaries, furnish the means to procure additional equipment, expand travel regions, and amplify promotional activities. Whatever the uses, to generate supplemental program finances, a coach or program administrator must apply the systematic foundations of management (Chapters 1-5: *Planning, Organizing, Human Resources, Leadership,* and *Control*) as they relate to and are focused on the endeavor of fundraising.

Fundraising Defined

Barron's Dictionary of Business Terms characterizes fundraising as "the effort to solicit contributions from individuals or organizations for the operation of nonprofit entities" (Friedman, 1987). For a lucrative fundraiser, a systematic approach should be developed, tested, and implemented. In most cases this undertaking of fund solicitation falls to the coach or program administrator.

Administrative Tip

The financial needs of the athletic program will dictate the fundraising plan that one should choose. Additionally, the choice of fundraising activities may also be driven by the long-term growth potential of some fundraising programs. Some fundraising programs take multiple applications, over years of use, to reach their maximum financial potential. Once these types of multiple programs get rolling, they typically accumulate far greater capability of making dollars for the program.

As the fundraiser and developmental leader, one has to recognize three specific areas of operation:

1. Organization of the fundraising staff under one's jurisdiction. This is accomplished by an organizational chart of committees, volunteers, and staff. Each individual position should have a detailed job description and area of accountability within fundraising operation.
2. Institutional public relations, which includes (but is not limited to) publications, media relations, and program goodwill.
3. Development of fundraising activities:
   a. Annual and capital campaigns
   b. D-base development for private gift support
   c. Methods of solicitation
   d. Maintenance record keeping

(Grasty and Sheinkept, 1982)

Annual and Capital Fundraising

There are two distinct and separate categories of fundraising. The first and most consequential is annual fundraising. The ultimate objective of an annual program is the maintenance and fortification of ongoing operations for the current season and fiscal year. Annual fundraising programs should fill the deficit between revenues generated and expenditures incurred. If the existing program is functioning at a net income (surplus funds or "in the black"), the prime utility of an annual program may be to upgrade and diversify services to the staff and players as well as to enlarge the volume of spectators through increased promotion.

In most not-for-profit ventures, annual fundraising is used to underscore sizable endowment campaigns. This fundraising effort concentrates on large philanthropic donations from a small number of individuals. While this approach is the most straightforward to track, it is also a tremendous gamble. For example, if a program has five principal benefactors and one or two of these individuals or organizations are unable to match their annual projected contributions, the program could immediately experience up to a 20-40% reduction in operational funds. From a risk averse perspective, a program that cultivates a broad base of donors and fundraising activities will experience far less financial impairment from smaller abstaining donations. This is not to argue in support of abandoning the large donors and sponsors, but rather to stress the monetary stability of a broad-based fundraising philosophy.

The principal difference between capital and annual fundraising is that the former is considered more of a perpetual, unending activity while the latter is an assignment-specific endeavor. Because of this element, the bigger the one-time donation, the better. Most capital fundraising programs have multimillion-dollar goals, characteristically within two to five years.

A special note relating to all fundraising activities, whether they are annual or capital in nature: There are two guiding principles that must be imparted to anyone associated with the program's fundraising.

1. No amount is too small.
2. Always personalize the "thank you" for the donation.

These are words to live by in fundraising.

Fundraising Programs and Activities

Figure 1: Fundraising Programs and Activities

Dream Actions

Construction Dedications

Luncheons/Dinners/Award Banquets

Deferred Gifts

Entertainment Programs

Product Sales

Direct Mail

In-Kind Trade

Publications

Phone Solicitations

The sections below clarify each fundraising activity's distinct advantages and disadvantages. They do so relying on or using a fairly abstract conceptual format. For the program's precise development and execution, fundraising ideas require open discussion by the coaches and staff to determine their operational feasibility.

Dream Auction (Annual or Capital)

Dream auctions are fundraising programs that are solo events that can be administered as one-time capital projects or annual events. Because of the amount of preparation, dream auctions are not suited to be recurrent fundraising endeavors. The program's basic structure is as follows:

1. The fundraising staff and volunteers solicit charitable gifts and services from local, regional, or even national businesses and corporations. For example, a local business or restaurant may donate a dinner for two, or a hair salon may contribute a free haircut. Rewards for the corporations and business entities who award products and services are beneficial; positive publicity as well as all donations are at cost and tax deductible. It should be distinguished for future reference that businesses are more likely to donate products rather than cash because products are valued at retail but have cash cost value at substantially lower amounts. Additionally, during the recruiting process,

Administrative Tip

There are some complexities in dealing with generous philanthropic donations and the individuals who bestow them. While these altruistic people are valuable to a program's funding, a coach or program administrator needs to take into account the desires and motivations behind their gifts. If their needs and motives are benevolent and sincere, work with these people to maintain their contributions and assistance. If a donor purpose and needs are not compatible with the program's operating philosophies, no matter how much money and backing is being offered, never sell the program's integrity.

the developmental staff should inaugurate an intense promotional campaign to publicize the event. All "blue chip" donations of products and services should be tied into promotion to gain interest and attendance at the event.

2. The affair, through a public auction format, barters and sells these gifts and services for auctioned values. For large auctions, it is advisable to enlist the aid of a professional auctioneer to facilitate the program. Another alternative is the concept of silent auctions, where items are displayed and people bid on them in an open format. Each item has a starting bid displayed and the participants has either tender offers through a lock box or via an exposed document list.

The realizable income from a prosperous dream auction is tremendous. The two functions of product or service solicitation and event promotion must be coordinated through the coach or program administrator. The promotional mix for this type of event can incorporate media advertising (e.g., newspapers, television, radio), direct target mailings, and personal invitations. The day event should have a meticulous itinerary and an itemized catalog of products and services to be auctioned. A pre-event reception is also recommended so patrons can browse and look at tangible items.

Construction/Brick Dedication (Capital)

For an enterprise (or in our case athletic program) that is constructing or has impending facility construction or renovation, the brick dedication fundraising program is an exceptional, high potential fundraising activity. The operation conditions:

1. For a predetermined price (usually in the region of $50.00 per brick), the fundraising committee solicits donations by selling bricks for the new or renovated facility. The program's paramount selling point is that each brick will have the donor's name (or tribute name) inscribed on it and it will be a permanent, visual component of the structure. The unit cost per brick with etching can be a minimal $5-10.00 per brick (depending on the construction type and quality).

2. For large donations, the contributor will have the opportunity to erect a facility plaque or a sectional dedication. Because this dedication has more logistical work associated with it, it is advisable to place a $500.00 minimum on this type of solicitation.

3. An extensive promotional program for this type of capital undertaking is a prerequisite. Community involvement is most important. Publicity and sales should be instituted at least two years in advance of ground breaking.

4. All sales have to be registered and mapped for future reference by donors. These maps should be as clearcut as possible to locate any and all dedications.

It should be noted that a vital first step before the program takes off is to get a definitive maximum number of bricks from the construction engineer that can be retailed. All public areas should be exactly measured and bricks to be used quantified.

The dimensions of capital funds raised by this fundraising strategy is constrained only by the size and the number of new or renovated facilities and the consolidated effort put into selling the bricks. For every new building, walkway, or public area under construction, a new brick dedication fundraising program could be instituted.

Luncheons/Dinners/Award Banquets (Annual/Capital)

Award banquets are fundraisers that are geared toward philanthropic recognition and appreciation as well as future charitable contributions. The foremost fundraising objectives are as follows:

1. For a first-time event, the honoring of a cherished individual, program, or holiday that can stimulate community enthusiasm and collaboration is imperative. Someone who is an affluent, steadfast supporter of the athletic program could be a recipient of an annual award. It is noteworthy to single out an event conscientiously without community overlap and antagonism.
2. A per-plate price is established. The price determination is based solely on the occasion and the value to the community. Benchmarking similar events by other organizations is a good starting point.
3. If possible, the event, which could be a yearly program or one-time activity, should be a black-tie affair with prominent community and nationally renowned speakers involved.

There are dangerous financial prospects associated with award banquets as fundraisers. First and foremost are the initial expenditures absorbed (upfront costs). Facility rental, music, food costs, and personnel can be exorbitant. Secondly, the event must be timed for maximum community participation. And finally, RSVP responses need to be tracked accurately and prioritized. One possible solution that could alleviate the inherent upfront monetary vulnerability of an awards banquet would be to have the projected expenses underwritten by a local or national corporation. For their participation, the company (or companies) will be the signature sponsors and will receive numerous publicity opportunities arising from the event.

Deferred Gifts (Wills and Bequests—Long-Term Fundraising)

Deferred gifts and endowments are more comparable to "planned gifts" than to special events and activities. Their goal is to transfer monetary gifts and pledged assets to an organization or program through fiduciary trusts, wills and endowments, insurance policies, and annuities. While this idea might seem a bit radical for a small athletic program, the long-term benefits of such solicitations are tremendously alluring. For example, endowed scholarships are directly related to wins and losses. They provide the athletes a program needs to compete. It should be noted that all types of deferred donations should be in conjunction with both parties' legal counsel and advisors.

Administrative Tip

For athletic programs with long histories, a Hall of Fame banquet ceremony can achieve two enormously notable fundraising purposes. First, the Hall of Fame event could be a profitable function within itself. Second, the individuals who are nominated and accepted into the Hall of Fame will then be vested members of the athletic program and will become likely future donors.

Entertainment (Annual)

Entertainment benefits as fundraising activities can incorporate an extensive variety of programs and applications. Because our athletics programs are by definition entertainment, we can concentrate our attention on something that we know quite well. From an athletics program standpoint, sponsoring instructional camps and clinics, indoor and outdoor tournaments, and pro and Olympic exhibitions are just a handful of the program-specific events that can be utilized as fundraisers. Nonathletic entertainment can encompass musical groups or singers, comedians, satirists, and featured speakers and lecturers.

Fundraising guidelines for this type of endeavor:

1. The development director must secure a suitable entertainer. Obviously, the more fashionable and popular the entertainer or entertainment, the easier it will be to acquire sponsorship and promotion. The entertainment should be (if possible) contracted by a net profit percentage. This will eliminate initial expenditures.

   Other costs could include advertising, facility rental, and event employees.

2. Advertising for this category of fundraising should be dynamic and intensive while at the same time community oriented. The acquisition of media coverage (through public relations, which is nonpaid advertising) should be optimized.

3. The realizable income is not only contingent on the entertainment, but also on the organization's commitment to the program. As with similar fundraisers, the predominant downside is the initial overhead costs and the risk of sparse attendance.

Product Sales (Annual)

Product sales are worthwhile fundraising activities for annual operations but are typically impractical for capital programs because of their limited financial potential. Underlying principles of product sales are as follows:

1. The fundraising director will contact a contingency sale/fundraising company. Articles to be sold can comprise clothing, candy, business paraphernalia, and personalized athletic items.

2. Because the sales are contingency supported, the program bears no liability for unsold products.

3. The sales force can be composed of designated internal stakeholders and selected external stakeholders. A targeted goal should be specified for each individual involved in the sales program. Sale incentives and awards can be employed to intensify participation and targeted goal achievement.

The principal disadvantages to contingency product sales are that they are fairly limited as fundraising activities due to the fact that most items being sold have a low retail value and the sales force is not trained in professional selling techniques and the commitment factor necessary for success is extensive. A profitable sales campaign involving 20 people could maximum out at around $3-5000.00. However, product sales are a creditable, rapid source of funds for program operations and are a way to harvest middle to lower socioeconomic community members.

Direct Mail

Direct mail is a superior mechanism for laying the groundwork for other fundraising tools and programs. But because of the low response rates associated with its operation (characteristically three to five percent on general mailings), it should not be retained as the athletic program's only organizational fundraising appliance. Its chief justifications and objectives are as follows:

1. The prime rationale for direct mailing is to indoctrinate and inform community members about program successes and fundraising goals. The solicitation of substantial funds is quite limited even with extensive volume mailing.

2. Each individual direct mailing must have a cost-benefit analysis done to determine its effectiveness in relation to its substantive costs. The cost elements of direct mailing are becoming a major ingredient in the utilization of this fundraising methodology. In other words, because of the continually increasing cost of postage, print work, and design, the athletic program must forecast the realizable earnings and evaluate whether the mailer is justified and cost sensible.

3. Products and materials for a bulk mailing must be engineered to be community relevant, to communicate the significance of the program and its fundraising considerations, to be straightforward and comprehensible, as well as to be rationally appealing, creative, and easy to respond to.

Direct mailers are typically time consuming in their production and entail having sizable mailing lists. Mailing lists, which can be from internal or external sources, are the most important component of direct mailing. A centralized, targeted listing can spell fundraising success, while poorly targeted listing will definitely spell failure.

To reiterate, one can cultivate the established, direct mailing operation by following the seven cardinal rules of direct mailing success:

1. Start with the objective of the direct mailing program.
2. Reach the right person on the right list.
3. Present the case in terms of benefits to the reader.
4. Use appropriate copy and layout.
5. Make it easy for the prospect to take action.
6. Tell the story over and over again.
7. Research the direct mailing efforts. (Grasty and Sheinkept, 1982)

Administrative Tip

Because of the volume of direct mail received by potential and current supporters, the program's direct mailing undertaking must be as distinctive and engaging as possible. Quality is typically the best way to differentiate the program's direct mail from other organization solicitations. Quality in direct mailing can be achieved through writing, construction, artwork, and assembly. If financially feasible, direct mail something of value to the prospective supporter. This tactic, while having a higher up-front costs associated with it (that is, monies that must be paid out before collecting any income), can drastically boost the response rate of the mailing.

Administrative Tip

When soliciting in-kind trades, underscore the fact that all in-kind trades are valued at retail but cost the donating organization purchased value. Also accentuate the possibility of substantial tax implications of retailed valued gifts.

Other Fundraising Activities (Annual/Capital)

In-Kind Trade

In-kind trade relies on an exchange of goods/services. The organization or program trades its product, service, or exposure opportunity for another organization's product or service. An example of an in-kind trade and exchange is an exchange of season tickets and advertising space in return for an automobile dealer vehicle. All trades should be value for value.

Publications

If the athletic program creates and distributes a media guide or visiting team travel guide, the sale of space inside these publications is a viable way to raise external funds. Businesses are reluctant to pay for advertising space. In-kind products for advertising space are a value-for-value bargain that will benefit both parties.

Phone Campaigns

As with direct mail campaigns, phone campaigns are limited fundraising activities due to the sheer number of phone solicitations individuals receive daily. Additionally, cold calling will have a much lower success rate compared to phone solicitations to a targeted, vested stakeholder group. Phone volunteers should work from a drafted script and should always remember that they are representatives of the program.

Summary

The aggregate number of fundraising programs accessible to an athletic program is only restricted by the resourcefulness and enthusiasm of the people involved. If the coach, as the program leader and fundraising director, has "bought into" the fundraising program and is committed, the rest of the staff will be committed. While fundraising activities can be difficult and a tremendous amount of hard work, they can have both extrinsic and intrinsic rewards. The extrinsic rewards from fundraising are simple: increased cash flow and operational funds. The intrinsic rewards from a successful fundraiser can range from providing others with enjoyment to the satisfaction of knowing that the program is being funded.

APPENDIX 11A: Action Outline for a Capital Fundraising Campaign

The following outline provides coaches and athletic program administrators with an action-oriented framework for a capital fundraising campaign. The outline is adapted from Thomas E. Broce's publication, *Fundraising: The Guide to Raising Money From Private Sources.*

I. Determination of relationship of capital campaign with overall fundraising program and activities
   A. Integration of campaign with all fundraising and promotional activities
   B. Coordination of campaign with annual fundraising programs
      1. Avoidance of simultaneous active fundraising efforts
      2. Identification of leaders and volunteers for campaign

II. Precampaign activities
   A. Planning by administration, operational personnel, and volunteers
   B. Prospect identification and evaluation
   C. Institutional factors effecting campaign
      1. Nature of organization/athletic department/club
      2. Location
      3. Economic factors affecting campaign (local and national)
      4. Campaign strengths
      5. Campaign weaknesses
   D. Case statement preparation (similar to mission statement)
      1. Program, projects, and objectives
      2. Justification of timing
      3. Vision, philosophy, and major goal of capital campaign
      4. Brief and comprehensible
      5. Compatible with other program missions
   E. Prospective cultivation
      1. Institutional interest
      2. Community contacts and special preprogram activities
   F. Precampaign education
      1. Participative climate
      2. Profile of present program and future aspirations
         a. Media relations
         b. News releases
         c. Institutional publications describing capital campaign goals
   G. Naming capital campaign
      1. Symbolic campaign
      2. Motivational
      3. Identifiable
   H. Campaign advertising
      1. Target toward prospective philanthropist
   I. Campaign leadership conference
      1. Educate fundraising staff and build campaign confidence and motivation

        a. Campaign steering committee
        b. Advisory board
        c. Special campaign chairpeople
    J. Promotional materials
        1. Newsletters
        2. Special presentations
        3. Video presentations
        4. Update reports
    K. Advance gift solicitation
        1. Timing
        2. Goal (20-40% of total)
        3. Sources
    L. Campaign kickoff
        1. Timed well after advanced gifts
        2. Appropriately announced
            a. Dinner/luncheons for campaign leaders
            b. Extensive media coverage
            c. Reiteration on goals and program objectives
III. Campaign organization
    A. Volunteers
        1. Well organized, trained, and motivated
            a. Effective size of aggregate group to reach goals
            b. Fundraising workshop
    B. Committees
        1. Policies communicated from program administrator
        2. Duties
            a. Direction of individual programs
            b. Supervision of volunteers
            c. Establishment of preapproved objectives
            d. Implementation of timetable
            e. Prospective donor evaluations
            f. Coordination and motivation of personnel under their supervision
            g. Establishment of quotas and schedules
            h. Identification and cultivation of major gifts
            i. Solicitation of intermediate gifts
            j. Responsible for mass solicitations
IV. Campaign operations
    A. Chief executive/program administrator
        1. Principle spokesperson
        2. Main attractant for major funding
    B. Developmental director and staff
        1. Manages staff
        2. Oversees and directs a majority of the campaign
        3. Committee leaders, operational personnel, and volunteer supervisor
        4. Campaign policies

5. Initiates promotional activities
6. Community assessment studies and prospect evaluation
7. Coordinates public relations
C. Campaign timetable
1. Practical and feasible
D. Solicitations
1. Personal
a. In person
b. By phone
2. Mail
a. Limited return
b. Directed to most likely prospects
c. Well planned and creative
3. Campaign packets
a. Key information summary
b. Question-and-answer format
c. Charts, graphs, and timetables for future objectives
d. Special brochure and regular program publications
V. Post-campaign activities
A. Acknowledgment of donors
1. During campaign
a. Private and public recognition
b. In-progress reports
c. News releases
d. General announcements
2. Continuing recognition
3. After campaign
a. Public announcements
b. Plaques and citations
c. Seek advice and council
d. Maintain contact
VI. Gift acknowledgment procedures
A. Systematic
1. Pledge records
2. Gift records
3. Gift acknowledgments
4. Billing reminders
B. Acknowledgments
1. Immediate
2. By letter and personal (when appropriate)
3. At special events and openings

Chapter 12 ....

Fundamentals of Risk Management for Athletics Programs

Objectives

- To highlight the magnitude of risk management issues for coaches and program administrators.
- To scrutinize the four major areas of sports risk management.
- To investigate facility and equipment risk management from a procedural and sensory perspective.
- To examine personnel risks.
- To assess the conditions for contractual agreements as well as areas of athletic program operation which necessitate contractual agreements.
- To appraise external risks from an insurance perspective.

Introduction

The issue of risk management in sports programs is an enormously detailed and specialized legal and financial field. Therefore, it is not the intention of this chapter to instantly make a coach or administrator a certified expert in risk management. However, it is an aspect of business about which we, as program managers, should be cognizant and have a fundamental working knowledge. We work with people in a service industry that is exceedingly physical and dynamic. Extensive travel is involved, numerous facilities are utilized, and we typically have a wide range of support staff

Administrative Tip

When dealing with risk and risk management, never take for granted that all parties involved with the program know the significance of good risk management policies. Assumptions are dangerous in any business situation, especially in the realm of sports program risk.

that requires supervision. It is necessary to persistently evaluate our program's environment and make the appropriate judgments to reduce the chance of risk and loss.

Risk Management Defined

The most reasonable definition for risk management is that it is "the concept of proactive efforts taken by a sports program/administrator to prevent losses" (Miller, 1997). Hearing the word *losses*, one might think of litigation through gross negligence. However, lawsuits can transpire over the slightest and most improbable incidents. Let's be honest in assessing our culture by stating that we exist in a "sue happy" society. Outrageous legal court settlements (whether warranted or not) are commonplace and coaches are as vulnerable as anyone.

The concept of risk management goes beyond gross negligence. In her text, *Sports Business Management*, Lori Miller categorizes risks into the following environmental segments:

1. Facility Risks/Equipment Risk
2. Personnel Risk
3. Contract Related Risk
4. External Risk

If coaches adopt her classifications and fashion them toward their individual sport, it will give them the basis for instituting a game plan of approaching and reducing program and personal liabilities. Will we ever eliminate risk? No. Risk is a concept of uncertainty. However, our objective should be to influence and manage as many variables as possible so that the likelihood of a detrimental and liable occurrence is diminished.

Facility and Equipment Risk

In reviewing conceivable facility and equipment risks, a coach or program administrator must first think of all the worst-case scenarios and, around them, all potential problems. The question that one must always ask is "What is the most catastrophic scenario?" In other words, a coach or program administrator must be a consistent and intentional observer of potential disasters. Facility and equipment deal with the physical aspects of our positions. They are tangible objects that our senses (seeing, hearing, tasting, touching, and smelling) can examine and evaluate. When assessing the condition, layout, and safety of existing (or potential) facilities and equipment, it is advisable to set aside separate, unencumbered time prior to facility and/or equipment usage and use utilizes one's senses to evaluate the situation. As we all know, once a scheduled activity begins, our heightened attention is more on that activity than the surroundings. As a result, the facility/equipment walk-through should be considerably in advance to circumvent any other distractions. For example, before commencing preseason training, set the gym, field, or facility up according to the precise practice requirements a day before starting. With the program's staff, do a safety walk-through. Use the five human senses and ask questions:

- How does the ground (floor) feel? Is it clean of miscellaneous items or does it need more attention?
- Is the light adequate enough to conduct practice?
- What is the facility temperature? Is there proper circulation?
- Is there proper spacing around the participation areas? If not, are the walls or boundaries padded to avoid injury?
- What is the condition of the operational equipment? Is it in good working order?
- What is the condition of the locker rooms? Is there an unhealthy smell? Is the locker room area secure?

Figure 1: Checklist for Controlling Premise Liability: Questions to Ask in a Premise Liability Audit (Jennings and Shippers, 1989)

1. Are there any standing pools of water (swimming pool, decorative pools, or the like)?
2. Are the walking areas adequately maintained? Check for. . .
   - Hazard areas or holes that might be walked into (level with sidewalk).
   - Evenness of walking areas.
   - Ice and snow.
   - Lighting problems.
   - Unidentified steps.
   - Things people could bump into, such as windows.
3. Are materials spilled? Where? Why?
   - Is there a policy on clean-up?
   - Is someone assigned to the task?
4. Are customers permitted or required to be in dangerous areas?
5. Where are the warning signs posted on the property? Are these habitually ignored?
6. Are nonparticipants creating hazards on the property?
   - Have there been thefts and crimes?
   - Do children regularly come on the property? Where? Does the property have any attractive nuisances?
   - Do nonparticipants use the property (roller skaters, bicyclists, etc.) in any way during business or nonbusiness hours? If so, who uses the property and how?
   - What other staff members besides the ones directly in the program use or maintain the facility?
7. Are there height dangers? Is there ready access to the roof?
8. What procedures are used to maintain the facility?
9. To what dangers are the employees (in our case staff and athletes) exposed? What safety equipment are they required to wear? Do they always wear it? Do they ever use equipment in an inappropriate way?
10. Have there been recent complaints about the premises? What were the procedures to handle those complaints? What were the results of those complaints?
11. What accidents have occurred on the premises in the last three years? What caused each? Did any result in legal actions? If so, what were the outcomes?
12. What procedures are established if an accident occurs in or around the facility?

- Does our current design of the field (court, gym) minimize the chance for injury?
- Where will the athletes obtain water? Could there unintentionally be a hazardous situation caused by its placement and distribution?

The Jennings and Shippers 1989 book *Avoiding and Surviving Lawsuits* has an outstanding checklist for controlling premise liability (Figure 1) as well as a four-step procedure to follow after an accident has transpired (Figure 2). These figures, in concert with the above questions, should provide one with information to proactively handle most facility risks.

Figure 2: Procedures After an Accident (Jennings and Shippers, 1989)

1. Arrange for medical care for the injured party and provide transportation or other assistance for relatives and friends.
2. Try to obtain the answers to the following questions:
   - Who was the injured party?
   - How long has the injured party been there?
   - Where was the injured party before he or she arrived on the premises?
3. If there are witnesses to the accident, get their names, addresses, and phone numbers as well as a brief statement from each.
4. Prepare a written accident report, including all the collected information as well as any additional thoughts or observations.

Administrative Tip

A coach or program administrator should never disregard any person's apprehension when it comes to the actual physical risks of the facility and equipment (no matter how trivial the impact might be). Address the concerns for impact and immediate legitimacy. Special note: Once an item has been brought to the attention of a manager or authority, the item then becomes that person's responsibility and he or she will be held accountable for it.

The aggregate number of questions to be asked will be based on the condition of the operational equipment or facility and the coaching staff's sensitivity to risk. Obviously, the newer the facility or equipment, the less one should worry about its structural condition rather than its continual upkeep. Even the newest facilities become hazardous without appropriate maintenance.

What if the program is dealing with a confined budget and older facilities and equipment? Critically document (in writing) all possible problems and legitimate concerns and give copies to the program's supervisor and/or the individual the program may be leasing the facility from. Make this correspondence as absolute, clear, and professional as possible. Declare facts, be very lucid, and eliminate all impulsive, emotional responses. Also, furnish solutions to all conclusions brought forth in the disclosure. Copy reports to all parties concerned. As unpleasant as this process sounds, by conferring any potential dangers, one has taken steps to limit personal liability.

Does this imply that the coach or program administrator should disregard potential problems and conduct activities as though there is nothing wrong? No. Sit down with the program's staff and athletes and candidly discuss potential facility and equipment risks. Make everyone mindful of the circumstances and incorporate a safety-sensitive theme into the program.

Personal Risk

A service industry is defined as "a type of business that sells assistance and expertise rather than a tangible product" (Friedman, 1987). In transforming this description to our profession, we as coaches and administrators provide assistance and expertise to our subordinates and players so they, in turn, can furnish the final consumer (fan) with an intangible service (entertainment). In other words, the nature of our business involves dealing with and training people internally so they can produce externally. This type of intense training mandates personnel policies and procedures to minimize risks.

In an ideal world, all men and women would work in a utopian environment of collaboration and cohesiveness. Personal and professional antagonism and conflicts among an organization's personnel would be nonexistent. Unfortunately, we do not inhabit or work in an idyllic world. As a coach and administrator, one needs to cultivate, motivate, and influence people (staff and players) to achieve the program's mission. This is the substance of personnel management.

Some of the issues facing business managers dealing with people:
* Fair hiring and recruiting policies
* Equal pay for equal work
* Sexual harassment

Administrative Tip

A subject that has become a central issue in sports programs is fan interaction with athletes and staff. Think of fan interaction as a personnel safety issue. Have policies and procedures in place to safeguard the program's people from outside contact.

Figure 3: Program Manual/Policies and Procedures

Mission Statement

Long-Term Objectives (3 to 5 Years—Both Athletically and Nonathletically)

Short-Term Objectives to Reach Long-Term Goals

Team Rules and Policies

Academics	Practices
Matches	Travel
Player Responsibilities	Player Rules

Disciplinary Policies

Staff Job Responsibilities

Head Coach/Administrator
Assistant Coaches
Trainers
Sports Information
Secretaries
Other Related Members

- Discriminatory hiring and employment practices
- Wrongful termination disputes
- Promotion and preferential treatment
- Valid, reliable evaluation methods
- Employee job safety

Do these uncertainties challenge coaches? Absolutely. In fact, coaches are confronted with these issues from two separate work groups: program players and staff/employees. Once again, the massive content of personnel management and the consequences involved in supervising people are beyond the scope of this text. However, there are some indispensable, common-sense measures a coach can adopt to create a more risk-averse personnel system. First of all, get educated (or reeducated) in prevalent personnel topics. Browse through human resource texts, attend human resource seminars (e.g., sexual harassment, discrimination, OSHA workshops), and revisit the organization's strategic personnel plan. Second, develop a program manual that spells out specific expectations for the program and its members. The program manual could be composed as in Figure 3.

Staff/Player Evaluation System

Systematically evaluate the program's staff and players (even if it is through scheduled verbal meetings). Give them an opportunity to voice their feelings and beliefs about any aspect of the program. Finally, maintain a file for each employee and player. Document all pertinent material for future reference. If feasible, have dates, times, and specific items recorded for reference purposes. This can reduce the possibility of any discrepancies and contradictions.

Contract-Related Risk

Administrative Tip

As stated, oral contracts and agreements are just as binding as written contracts. To enforce oral contracts and agreements, with the permission of all parties concerned, tape the oral contract.

The importance of contracts can be summed up in the following excerpt:

> It is impossible to overestimate the importance of the contract in the field of business. Every business entity, whether large or small, must necessarily enter into contracts with its employees, its suppliers, and its customers in order to conduct business operations. (Smith and Robinson, 1985)

Contracts deal categorically with rights, responsibilities, and remuneration (compensation) among participants. The fundamental requirements for a contractual agreement (whether formal and written or informal) are listed in Figure 4.

Agreement, Consideration, Contractual Capacity, and Legality are formally known as *elements of a contract*. The last two are possible defenses to the information or the enforcement of a contract.

It is meaningful to note that once these six criteria are met, an oral contract is just as binding as a written one. The conspicuous disadvantage is that oral transactions are much harder to enforce precisely because it is

Figure 4: Requirements for a Contract (Miller and Jentz, 1999)

Requirements for a Contract

Agreement

An agreement includes an offer and acceptance. One party must offer to enter into a legal agreement and another party must accept the terms of the offer.

Consideration

Any promise made by parties must be supported by legal sufficient and bargained for consideration (something of value received and promised to convince a person to make a deal).

Contractual Capacity

Both parties entering into the contract must have the contractual capacity to do so; the law must recognize them as possessing characteristics that qualify them as competent parties.

Legality

The contracts purpose must accomplish some goal that is legal and not against public policy.

Genuineness of Assent

The apparent consent of both parties must be genuine.

Form

The contract must be in whatever form the law requires; for example, some contracts must be in writing to be enforceable.

harder to prove their existence. That is why it is strongly recommended to formalize all contracts in writing.

Among coaches and administrators, contracts can be applied comprehensively to minimize personal and program risks. Unless one is a contract lawyer, it is important to mention that the more critical a contractual arrangement the more apropos it is to involve an independent specialist in contract law. For example, if a coach is in a position to negotiate a long-term employment contract (which most of us would regard as a considerable employment item), it is advisable to get a contract lawyer to counsel one as to the rights and responsibilities of the contractual obligations. On the other hand, there are contractual arrangements that in everyday program operations do not necessitate legal representation and advisement to execute. The following are a few examples.

Program Purchasing

When interacting with vendors, it is prudent to obtain written quotes on all services and products when negotiating prices, quantities, and specifications. After both parties stipulate the services/products to be included, formal written contracts (and purchase orders if applicable) should be gen-

Administrative Tip

With any substantial program purchase, have the quotes and estimates evaluated by the program's legal counsel. Specify all the program's purchasing requirements, and have the legal advisor verify that these stipulations are included in the contractual purchase agreement.

erated and approved by all parties. Keep copies of all documentation for future reference.

Team/Personal Travel

Maintaining comprehensive files for each trip planned and completed is essential. Files should consist of hotel contracts, rental vehicle contracts, flight receipt stubs, and competition contracts. If the organization pays a contract in advance, make a copy of the check for tangible proof of the program's fulfillment of the bilateral agreement.

Booster Clubs

If one's club or school has a booster association, generate a contractual arrangement for its enrollment. These contracts should spell out the benefits of membership as well as the financial requirements of the patrons and boosters.

Summer Camps

To minimize disorder, keep all camp business and contracts separate from normal program operations. Contracts for insurance, staff employment, state registrations, camper registration, camper insurance and medical documentation, and checking accounts are among some of the contracts that should be formalized and retained.

Scholarships

In a collegiate situation, the actual paperwork for scholarships is traditionally produced by members of the school's financial aid department. Each coach should discuss final arrangements with each player while hand-delivering (if feasible) the scholarship contract. This will prevent possible miscommunications and grievances. Keep copies of the scholarship contracts in each player's program file for future reference.

External Risk

External risks are environmental elements outside the control of the operation and program coach or administrator. The question then arises: If the external risks are outside our control, why do we need to acknowledge them or be preoccupied with them? This is where the concept of adaptation versus control separates the prosperous, long-term managers from the day-to-day operators. If one's managerial objective to minimize risk, one should proactively adapt the program to environmental elements that affect the business but are out of one's immediate power to control or change.

In strategizing for external risk, one must be future oriented. For example, if the country is suddenly in an economic downturn that alters the business operations, the most enviable strategy would have been to anticipate this direction and retool the enterprise in advance to compensate and adapt. Unfortunately, some predicaments are simply unpredictable. The key element in successfully managing these circumstances is to try to fore-

Administrative Tip

Have sufficient copies of all team travel contracts available for all program staff members. This can provide program travel safety as well as planning flexibility.

Administrative Tip

Most sports governing bodies require detailed record maintenance when operating sport-related instructional camps. Make sure all contractual forms are readily retrievable in case of a spot audit.

Administrative Tip

As with all contractual arrangements, shop around for the optimum insurance policy. Remember to never sacrifice the quality of coverage for a better cost. Money saved now could be money paid later.

cast whether they are stable and likely to remain or transient and likely to change. If a coach or program administrator can foresee the situation becoming a permanent trend, then he or she needs to adapt the program's operations as quickly as possible and proactively "get out in front" of circumstances. Another solution to unforeseen events is to have an insurance arrangement that can protect the program, facilities, and so on.

The anticipatory use of insurance (for all levels of operation, not just external risk) is essential in today's coaching and program administration environment. The 1989 text, *Legal Handbook for Small Businesses,* has a four-item checklist on insurance selection and strategies. The following is an adaptation.

Figure 5: Insurance Strategy (Lane, 1989)

1. Prepare an inventory of all exposures.
2. Note which hazards can be reduced by precautionary measures, with estimate costs of each measure.
3. Determine whether specific or blanket insurance might protect the program at a lower cost than the precautionary measures.
4. If the insurance cost is only slightly better than the cost of the precautionary measures, consider whether the value of one's time in processing insurance claims is likely to equal or exceed the marginal cost advantage for the insurance.

Determination of the level of insurance protection that the program will need once again relates to the coaches/program administrators own personal perspective of risk and liability.

Summary

One of the central objectives of the book is to enable the reader to become a critical thinker in the area of sports administration. No topic exemplifies this underlying premise as much as risk management. As coaches and program managers, our core concentration must be a philosophy of athlete and program safety. Athlete safety can be maintained through monitoring risks to facilities, equipment, and personnel. Program safety is through the committed monitoring of contractual agreements and the regulation of external risks through insurance. No matter what theme of risk administration a coach accentuates, he or she must be as thorough and detailed oriented as possible. Additionally, a coach or program administrator needs to enlist others in the process of risk management. The better the collective input, the better the potential hazards can be managed.

Chapter 13 ....

Strategic Management and Coaching

Objectives

- To describe the advanced business science of strategic management.
- To present a graphic depiction of the strategic management process.
- To dissect the business concept of SWOT analysis.
- To analyze the Five Forces Model of Competitive Analysis as it relates to coaching and program administration.
- To consider the internal Generic Building Blocks of Competitive Advantage as they relate to athletic programs.
- To offer an overview of other generic strategic management concepts that can be utilized by coaches and program administrators.

Introduction

The foundations of management discussed in Chapters 1 - 5 (*Planning, Organizing, Human Resource Management, Leadership,* and *Control*) are the primary building blocks of a solid business and athletic program. Strategic management, the next level beyond these indispensable functions, deals strictly with competitive positioning, critical operational analysis, and maximizing the program's internal resources and capabilities. This chapter elaborates on some of the predominant strategic management business concepts as they pertain to coaching and athletic program administration.

Administrative Tip

Strategic management, more than any other business function, is connected with independent and critical thought. Most decisions that one makes as a coach or program administrator involve the replication of a previous decision. Strategic management is a more creative mindset. Recognize those decisions that are no-brainers and those that take strategic reflection.

Strategic Management Defined

There are numerous interrelated interpretations of the business science of strategic management. Two such definitions that encompass the essential nature of strategic management are as follows:

1. "Strategic management is the ongoing process of ensuring a competitive superior fit between an organization and its changing environment. . . it is a pattern of decisions and a product of actions and results" (Kreitner, 1995).

2. "Strategic management is the process of planning a firm's long-term course of action, managing its comprehensive resources, and fulfilling its mission within a broad environment" (Holt, 1990).

From these two explanations, one can understand that strategic management is the competent utilization of an athletic program's assets (whether tangible resources such as cash and facilities or intangible capabilities such as staff skills and knowledge), which leads the program to sustaining, and even increasing, its competitive strength and position. In the simplest terms, strategic management deals with how one can compete with and (hopefully) surpass the competition.

Formulation of Strategic Management

In his 1994 manuscript, *The Rise and Fall of Strategic Planning*, Henry Mintzberg designs a model of the strategic management planning process. Figure 1 is a graphic depiction of his work.

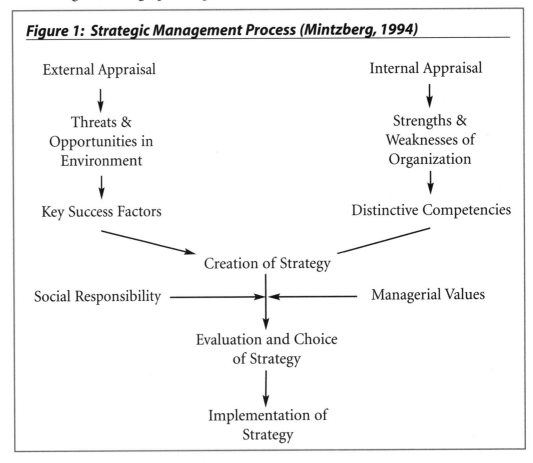

Figure 1: Strategic Management Process (Mintzberg, 1994)

This progressive model goes from where the program is to where the program needs to be. The first step is to assess the prevailing situation from an internal and an external perspective. Internally, one needs to perform a strength and weakness investigation. Very similar to the pro and con assessment, an internal strength and weakness evaluation looks critically at the athletic program's operations. The key word is "critically." Contemplate every component of the athletic program and consider whether it is a strength (operational asset) or a weakness (operational liability). It is advisable to start the strength/weakness appraisal process by prioritizing (or inventorying) the most crucial factors of the program's operation to the least consequential components. Hopefully, when the evaluation is completed, the most notable and significant operational elements will be predominantly considered strengths. A coach's or program administrator's philosophy in converting the internal analysis to strategizing should be to always maximize strengths and minimize weaknesses (or even convert weaknesses to strengths).

The second step in exploring where the program is in relation to where it needs to be is an external analysis or an opportunity/threat study. This process essentially audits all of the external environmental factors that affect the program's operation to determine if they are possibilities for growth and competitive advantage or threats to the program. Once again, prioritize the environmental elements from the most significant to the least notable. If one is fortunate, opportunities will outweigh threats. A coach's philosophy in this external analysis should be to exploit opportunities and fortify the program against threats.

To strategize from the strengths/weaknesses and opportunities/threats stage (also known as SWOT analysis) is straightforward logic. The best-case scenario is that the athletic program has a distinct strength that can be used to exploit an external opportunity. At the other end of the spectrum, the program might have a prominent weakness that coincides with an external threat. As the program administrator, one's obligation is to look at each external element as it relates to the internal operational strengths/weaknesses.

There are four primary scenarios.

Strength——————————Opportunity

Take advantage of one's supremacy in the situation and strategize the exploitation of the opportunity

Strength——————————Threat

In this proposition, the program should be able to counteract this distinctive danger.

Weakness——————————Opportunity

This condition needs a resolution. Does the program eliminate the weakness to take advantage of the circumstance or does it pass on the opportunity? Remember, this predicament is potentially dangerous. If the program passes on the opportunity and the program's competition takes advantage of the contingency, it might then become a distinct threat.

Weakness——————————Threat

Administrative Tip

Another way to conceptualize SWOT analysis is to maximize the program's internal strengths, minimize the program's internal weaknesses, exploit the program's external opportunities, and defend against the program's external threats.

This condition typically requires prompt action. The more hazardous and powerful the threat, the more immediate and decisive is the need to respond to it.

At this point, the program administrator needs to put together the program's strategies based on the prior analysis. When constructing them, follow these simple rules:

1. Strategy formulation should be a controlled, conscious process of thought.
2. Responsibility for the process rests with the chief executive [in our case, coach or administrator].
3. Strategy formulation should be simple and informal.
4. Strategies should come out of the design process.
5. Strategies should be explicit and, if possible, articulated.
6. Strategies should be unique.
7. Only when strategies are fully formulated, should they be implemented. (Mintzberg, 1994)

Two more areas in Mintzberg's model that need to be briefly discussed are *social responsibilities* and *manager values*. After a strategy is formulated, but preceding its implementation, a coach or program administrator needs to question it from an ethical and social context as well as from his or her own inner values and the philosophical values of the program. Both of these issues will be discussed in more detail in Chapter 14, *Business Ethics and Coaching*.

Administrative Tip

To manipulate the Five Forces Model components, an athletic program must have strong core competencies. Core competencies equate to the internal abilities, skills, resources, and talents of the organization. Simply put, to control the external elements one should have a formidable internal foundation.

Five Forces Model

As one of the country's foremost theorists in strategic management, Michael Porter has numerous models and theories in contemporary administration and management. Two of his most universally applicable and complementary models are the Five Forces Model, which probes an industry's five principal external components, and the Generic Building Blocks of Competitive Advantage (discussed immediately after this section), which examines an organization's internal operations.

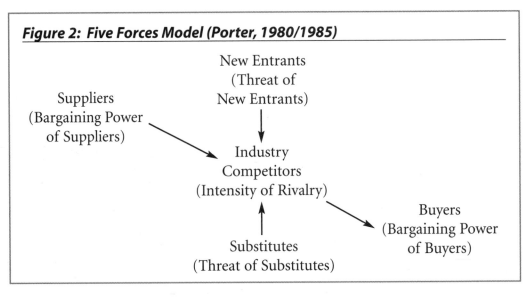

Figure 2: Five Forces Model (Porter, 1980/1985)

New Entrants
(Threat of
New Entrants)

Suppliers
(Bargaining Power
of Suppliers)

Industry
Competitors
(Intensity of Rivalry)

Buyers
(Bargaining Power
of Buyers)

Substitutes
(Threat of Substitutes)

As previously stated, the Five Forces Model is a theoretical representation that delves into the five foremost external components in an industry. In our case, our industry is athletics. To adapt this concept, we must take the comprehensive categories given by Porter and focus them on our particular programs.

Additionally, before we elaborate on each individual factor of the model, it must be emphatically stated that the more influence a component has on our operations, the more of a danger it is to our programs. Conversely, the weaker (or more influence we have on the force), the more possibility we have for opportunities.

Power of Suppliers

As we go around the model, the first external segment that needs to be analyzed is the bargaining power of suppliers. Clearly stated, suppliers furnish the inputs for our organization's outputs. In fashioning this to athletic programs, our output is our team's performance. What are the inputs to produce that output? Our staff, athletes, specialized equipment, etc. To illustrate, for all of us the most significant input to produce our output must be accomplished, quality athletes. From there, ask some of these elementary questions:

- Who provides our athletes?
- Do they control our working association or do we?
- Do we need to pursue them or do they approach us?

In almost every sport, athletic programs are divided into strata or tiers. If one's program is classified as a tier-one program (which has a high profile and a commanding history of achievement and exposure), the coach or program administrator can characteristically dominate the relationship with the suppliers of the program's athletes. The coach will have, in most cases, the opportunity to "pick and choose" from the elite feeder programs and suppliers. However, if one's athletic program is a lower tier (profile, lower/less funding, etc.), dealing with the suppliers of athletes takes on an altogether different viewpoint. Analyze all of the inputs into the program from this vantage and formulate the input strategies from there.

Back to our example: If the program is not an upper-tiered program, what strategies can one use to obtain the elite athlete? What strengths can be emphasized and weaknesses minimized to secure the talent? The less power the program has, the more creatively one needs to strategize.

Bargaining Power of Buyers

As program administrators, this exterior determinant relates to funding. Funding from ticket sales or donations are two such dominant components. Along the same thoughts as our prior example, if the program is a tier-one program that has elite athletes and a solid track record, in most cases, ticket sales or fundraising activities are a distinct opportunity. Once again, if the program is a lower strata program, an inability to find supporters and fans could be a consequential program threat. One's method of support procurement would in most cases need to be inventive and continuous.

Substitutes

The concept of substitutes relates to the convenience and accessibility of other products that the consumer can use instead of your organization's product. In our situation of athletics, fan support of the program is analogous to consumer support of a business product. For example, if one's athletic program and team are located in a region where there are a limited number of other sports programs or athletic events, then direct substitutes would be less of a threat to the program's fan base. On the other hand, if one's program is located in an area with abundant substitute athletic programs and events, fan support (as well as program publicity and interest) would be a more tenuous issue. Additionally, if the athletic program is located inside an overall athletic department (one of several teams inside an academic institution), then internal substitutes are also an issue a coach would need to address for funding, staff, and fan endorsement.

Another area that was previously discussed that might preoccupy a coach is the acquisition of athletes. If recruited talent has an option of participating in other sports instead of the program's sport, this is an input substitute that will need a strategic response. To distinguish all of the possible substitutes to the program, inventory all of the principal components of the program, prioritize those elements, and precisely examine each for the danger of substitutes. The more meaningful and significant the ingredient of the program, the more the coach or program administrator will need specific actions to minimize the affects of any possible substitutes.

Rivalry Among Existing Firms and Programs

This classification is the most discernible and tangible of the Five Forces Model. Our immediate competition is the one strategic element we as coaches tend to be mindful of. Our output and results are a direct reflection of our competitors' output and results. The stronger or more potentially strong each of our direct competitors is, the more of a threat that competitor is. The same format for strategizing can be utilized in this category. List all of the program's legitimate competitors, prioritize them by competitive potency, then develop strategies to competitively perform against each. Additionally, do an internal strength/weakness appraisal of each competitor to form a more effectual strategy.

New Entrants

The final broad segment in Porter's model that we can adapt to athletic programs is the examination of potential new competitors entering our external environment. In other words, who has the capacity to penetrate our competitive environment and what do they "bring to the table"? New entrants can be start-up athletic programs with no prior history or they can be from established organizations trying to expand into different arenas. By far, this category is the most difficult to predict. Suppliers, buyers, competitive rivals, and substitutes are already existing components that are tangible in nature and grounded in reality. New entrants require more guesswork and anticipation because of uncertainty.

In investigating this classification of the model, one needs to comprehend the concept of *barriers to entry*. The higher the barriers the more difficult it would be for a new competitor to penetrate the program's competitive environment. The opposite is also true: The lower the barriers, the more of a danger new entrants can be to the program. What are some of the barriers that sports programs might encounter? The first and foremost is the financial obligation to break into the competitive environment. Another barrier could be the governing bodies' licenses, charters, or organizational restrictions and regulations. For example, the barriers to entry into the National Football League are uncommonly high. The NFL has exorbitant financial as well as regulatory barriers. On the other hand, an individual who might want to establish a youth sports program would encounter low barriers, such as minimal restrictions from a governing body and moderate financial commitment. To strategically dissect this section of the model, define all of the barriers to entry, then recognize who could fulfill these requirements, then, finally, determine if they will enter the program's competitive environment.

Generic Building Blocks of Competitive Advantage

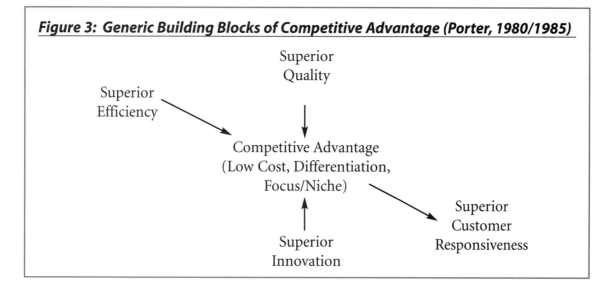

Figure 3: *Generic Building Blocks of Competitive Advantage (Porter, 1980/1985)*

Porter's second consequential theory that can be related to strategic management of athletic programs is the Generic Building Blocks of Competitive Advantage. While the preceding Five Forces Model dealt with exploring outside environmental factors for opportunities and threats, this model investigates an organization's internal components and philosophies as they coincide with assessing its strengths and weaknesses. The positions a program takes—both philosophically and in substantive actions toward the four major elements of superior quality, superior innovation, superior efficiency, and superior customer responsiveness—all lead to an overall strategic game plan for a competitive advantage (differentiation, low cost, niche/focus).

In the simplest terms, how we operate internally will furnish us with our strategies to compete externally. It should be emphasized that a program must predetermine its philosophical base toward the four generic building blocks before it can structure and implement its discernible goals, strategies, and actions.

Superior Efficiency

The concept of efficiency deals strictly with the transformation of a program's inputs to produce a program's outputs. In analyzing this classification ask, What are our inputs/resources and how are we using our capabilities and expertise to make the best product (output)? Acutely probe each resource and observe it from a strength/weakness standpoint to see how well it is managed. The general business statement that encompasses the essence of efficiency: *Because resources are limited, the less input used to produce a* high *quality output the more efficient the program.* Remember, maximize the program's inputs but never sacrifice high quality.

Superior Quality

Quality is a complicated concept that has quantitative, numerical elements as well as qualitative, subjective aspects. It is also an abstraction that is determined introspectively by the coaching staff in addition to externally by the program's customers. To explain: In business, quantitative quality measurements can simply coincide with the number of units being sold or the number of reworks being returned. In athletic programs, the fundamental measure of quality is wins-losses. However, in both business and athletics, quality also has people's sentiments and convictions associated with it. Both go hand-in-hand. How people subjectively feel about a product is typically linked to the quantity sold. Who determines the level of quality the program generates? It will ultimately be the people who use the product and fund the program. They will tell all stakeholders in no uncertain terms if the quality is good or not by their support. Be proactive. Ask customers, fans, and athletic administrators what level of quality they desire and expect. The prevailing business statement that describes quality: *Overwhelm the customer with quality.* This, in turn, will increase the program's support and funding as well as determine who wants to be involved in the program.

Superior Customer Responsiveness

This category of the generic building blocks model can be summed up with a succinct, lucid statement: *The customer is everything.* No matter what business or program, this declaration of customer satisfaction coming first and foremost should be the substructure of every aspect of the organization. Forgetting it will cause almost inescapable failure. If one does not satisfy the needs of customers and supporters, the competition most unquestionably will. One must ask questions:

- Who are our customers?
- Who are our supporters?

- What do they want and what do they require?
- Do our planned goals, strategies, and actions always provide customers and supporters with the greatest possible output and the highest conceivable satisfaction?
- How do they want our output and performance?
- When do they want it?
- Where do they want it?
- Why are they supporters of our program?
- Is customer satisfaction accomplished through providing the highest quality product? Is there an unconditional commitment to quality throughout our organization?
- Does the competition supply more customer and supporter satisfaction?
- What does the competition do that we have the capability of imitating to increase supporter satisfaction?

The list of questions is extensive.

Superior Innovation

In today's business world, innovation characteristically relates to technological advancements in improving the production process or the actual product itself. We can fashion this to athletic programs by correlating innovation in the production process to new, internal training techniques and innovation in the product/output to new performance tactics. Does one's sport lend itself to supplementary and innovative training techniques? Is the program's sport one that is evolving? Is the sport conducive or receptive to new-fashioned and enhanced performance tactics? The strength-weakness evaluation of superior innovation relates to the coaching staff's ability to learn and create.

After the four internal components of superior quality, efficiency, innovation, and customer satisfaction are scrutinized, Porter then stresses that from a strength-weakness evaluation in each category, one must choose a competitive strategy (or competitive philosophy) from the following three choices: differentiation, low cost, or focus niche. Griffin defines each of these:

> Differentiation: A strategy in which an organization wishes to distinguish itself from its competition through the quality of its products and services.
> Overall Cost Leadership/Low Cost: A strategy in which an organization attempts to gain a competitive advantage by reducing its cost below the costs of competing firms.
> Focus/Niche Strategy: A strategy in which an organization concentrates on a specific regional market, product line, or group of buyers (Griffin, 1996).

Once again, modifying these three overall philosophical strategies to athletic programs is easy. Athletic programs that have strengths in relation to their uniqueness of quality, innovation, efficiency, or customer satisfaction can develop and implement a differentiation strategy. In other words, sell the program to all conceivable supporters on distinctiveness and superiority over the competition. Try to equate unrivaled strengths with the factors that electrify supporters. On the other hand, if after the analysis of the four internal elements, one concludes that the athletic program is, in general, nondistinctive and can do little (at this time) to truly segregate itself from its competition, a low-cost strategy of underselling the competition could be embraced to generate support and funding. The final strategy of focus-niche essentially takes the program's specialized strengths and focuses them on a limited target market category for support. If the program's target market group of supporters has potential for growth, this strategy is exceptional for smaller and emerging programs.

In their 2001 text, *Strategic Management: An Integrated Approach*, Hill and Jones discuss the jeopardy of being "stuck in the middle" of one of these three strategies. The following is an extrapolation of their concerns.

> Each generic strategy requires a company to make a consistent choice in establishing a competitive advantage. . . [A] company must achieve a fit among one of the three possible strategies and must maintain its commitment to it. (Hill and Jones, 2001)

In other words, as the athletic administrator, one must match the operations with one of the three possible strategic scenarios and stick primarily with that approach. Jumping from strategy to strategy negatively affects internal focus as well as conveying an outwardly confused identity. This does not mean that a coach or program administrator should retain the chosen strategy after there have been internal or external changes. By all means, choose the most effectual strategy for the circumstances (and change in the operating situation). However, once you make that determination, be resolute and diligent in its application.

Other Strategic Management Concepts and Terminology

The subsequent concepts are general strategic management representations that need an abbreviated explanation. These concepts are in no special order or priority.

Groupthink

The designation *groupthink* "describes a mode of thinking that people engage in when seeking agreement becomes so dominant in a group that it tends to override the realistic appraisal of alternative problem solutions" (Certo, 1994). As a strategic manager, a coach/program administrator must balance the need for group cohesion with the avoidance of groupthink. Developing an atmosphere of cooperation with incisive, constructive input is the fundamental strategic goal.

Contingency Planning

Contingency planning is a deliberate attempt to develop other strategies to be ready for potential circumstances. Also known as *scenario planning*, this strategic management technique looks at conceivable and impending changes, and attempts to prepare the organization for them. All conceivable future circumstances need to be planned for. For example, even if one planned course of action is estimated at 60% certainty, while another is only 40% likely, the second would warrant almost as much serious attention as the first. However, if there is a likelihood of a future event/scenario with only a 10% chance, then having a preliminary plan would be more appropriate.

Strategic Groups

A strategic group within an industry is defined as "a select group of direct competitors who have similar strategic profiles within an industry" (Wright, Pringle, and Knoll, 1994). With this denotation, sports programs must define their closest competitors (for example, within the same division, conference, etc.) and develop front-line competitive strategies to challenge them first before expanding into other competitive environments.

Strategic Benchmarking

Benchmarking is observing other successful programs to emulate their techniques, capabilities, resources, and all other aspects that make them successful. Strategic benchmarking requires the following:

1. Identify what to benchmark. Choose activities that are crucial to competitive advantage.
2. Identify who to benchmark.
3. Measure the program's performance.
4. Identify specific programs and practices to adopt.
5. Develop an implementation plan. (Hindle, 1994)

The Law of Diminishing Returns

The Law of Diminishing Returns states that after a point there is less and less return for more and more effort. In athletic programs, the classic example of this is the overtraining conundrum. The more one trains and puts effort into producing a superior output, the worse the performance. As a coach, one must gauge how much is enough and how much is too much.

Learning Curve and Staff/Athlete Retention

The interpretation of the learning curve relates to the idea that the more repetition and times an employee (in our case, staff or athlete) does a particular task, the more competent he or she will become. Eventually, the learning curve will bottom-out due to the unmistakable fact that we, as humans, can only go as physically fast as our bodies and capabilities allow. Strategically, employee retention directly relates to the costs associated with the learning curve. The more one can maintain and retain staff members and players, the more the program can profit from premium productivity. Every time a new staff member or athlete joins the program, productivity will drop until he or she gets up to speed and produces at the level of proficient staff and athletes.

Outsourcing

Outsourcing is the process of subcontracting services, operational activities, and supplies that become an ingredient of the production process and/or final product. The questions to ask when considering outsourcing: Can this outsourcing organization or individual do it more inexpensively, faster, or better than us? Can the energy and time that we conserve with outsourcing provide us with a competitive advantage? It should be noted that

> the process typically begins by identifying the core value creation activities and to keep performing these activities within the organization. The remaining activities are reviewed to see whether they can be performed more effectively and efficiently by independent suppliers/outsourcing business. (Hill and Jones, 2001)

The rationale behind outsourcing is to ensure that the program will not rely on outside entities for core functional activities that have a major impact on success and survival.

Summary

The main functional goal of the business of strategic management is to provide a coach or program administrator with the tools to achieve a superior competitive advantage. In other words, for a coach to cultivate and maintain a viable, competitive advantage, he or she must consciously become a strategic futuristic thinker. The strategic determination process is systemized through theories such as SWOT analysis, the Five Forces Model, and the Internal Building Blocks of Competitive Advantage. These concepts will not only delineate macro, long-term organizational strategies, but will define day-to-day, micro functional actions.

Chapter 14 ....

Business Ethics and Coaching

Objectives

- To isolate individual influences on ethics.
- To elucidate the universal, ethical decision-making process.
- To equate the areas of ethical decisions in business management and athletic program administration.
- To describe the four social and ethical choices available to a coach or program administrator.
- To exhibit the 10 core values of an organization's code of ethics.
- To outline an ethical program plan.

Introduction

From the onset, it must be emphatically stated that this chapter is not written to lecture or to righteously pronounce what behaviors are right or wrong in a particular coaching or administrative situation. Additionally, this chapter is not designed to state how everyone should conform to certain professed norms of behavior. The purpose of this chapter is to lay the groundwork for understanding business ethics (and ethical behavior) as it relates to our profession: coaching and program administration. As one will see, business and personal ethics are extremely complex and subjective components in each of our lives.

Administrative Tip

Decisions have ramifications, no matter what program type—routine, strategic, or ethical. When a decision heavily involves ethical consideration, a coach or program administrator's resolutions will be more closely scrutinized. In making ethical decisions, one must think through all the potential ramifications of one's actions.

Individual Influences on Ethics

Ethics is a multidimensional concept that can be examined from an individual, organizational, or cultural perspective. The philosophical literature devoted to the subjects of ethics and values is staggering. However, for our purposes, we must start by asking what factors influence an individual's decision-making and ethical conscience. "An individual's personal code of ethics is influenced by four factors: family and peers, experiences, situations, and values" (Griffin and Ebert, 1993).

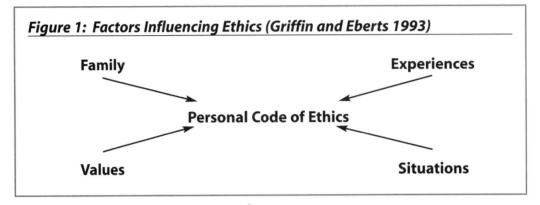

Figure 1: Factors Influencing Ethics (Griffin and Eberts 1993)

A key observation to note is that while each of these factors is more dominant in different life stages, they are all interrelated and continual throughout the life process. In an individual's formative years, family and peers are the most potent influences in developing an ethical foundation. During this period, most ethical judgments are supported, guided, and monitored by family members and friends. As one becomes more autonomous, personal experiences and situations dominate one's ethical development. Finally, values, which are influenced by a particular profession, organization, or culture/subculture group, affect the choices and beliefs in what behavior should be adopted. Through these elements, each one of us develops our own perception of reality. This is why introspective values and ethics vary enormously from individual to individual.

The Four-Step Ethical Decision-Making Process

From there, each of us goes through a four-step process for each ethical decision.

Step 1: This step basically asks the question, "Who will this decision effect?"

Step 2: This step is the internal evaluation of a decision and situation. Simply, what internal factors will one reference to evaluate the decision and situation?

Step 3: Moral intent is the evaluation step of looking at the surroundings (whether personal or professional) and assessing if the decision is ethical from other stakeholders' perspectives. This is the step that relates to moral intent/philosophy of the program environment.

Step 4: The final step is the action (or lack of action) step. Example questions:

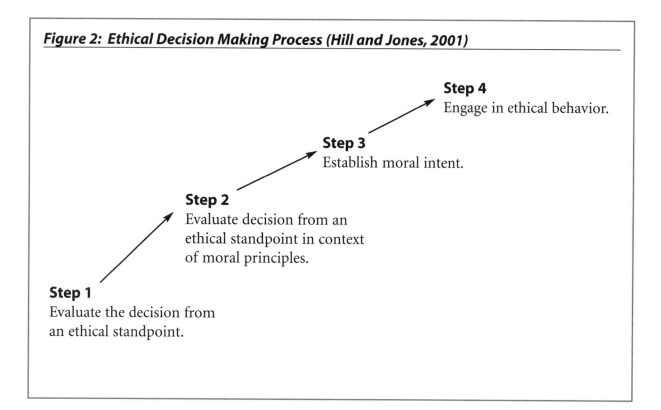

Figure 2: Ethical Decision Making Process (Hill and Jones, 2001)

Step 4
Engage in ethical behavior.

Step 3
Establish moral intent.

Step 2
Evaluate decision from an ethical standpoint in context of moral principles.

Step 1
Evaluate the decision from an ethical standpoint.

Do I engage in the activity? Do I react to an ethical situation? What decision do I make?

It should be noted that sometimes this four-step process is instantaneous. The more consequential the decision or situation, the more deliberation and time allotted. Additionally, the consideration of whether a situation/decision is consequential varies from person to person.

Business Ethics and Coaching

We as coaches are managers in the business of athletics. No matter at what level the program operates, the coach or program administrator is bound by the indispensable concepts of sound business practice. Nearly all the rationale that applies to traditionally conceived business ventures applies to our profession. Believing this is crucial in developing a successful and ethical program.

With that in mind, we need to recognize how today's businesses confront and tackle the increasingly important issue (and, often, dilemma) of ethical behavior. Business ethics is defined as "the principles of conduct within an organization that guide decision making and behaviors" (David, 1997). In other words, how do the organization and its people make determinations in difficult (sometimes impossible) situations? There is a remarkable similarity between the ethical circumstances that traditional business ventures and coach or program administration deal with. The following chart outlines the similarity between these two situations.

Administrative Tip

The stance the program takes with regards to social/ethical choices sets the tone for the program's in-house operations and external program perceptions. When a program acts in a dubious social/ethical way, it typically becomes very difficult to transform people's opinions and reactions to the program later on.

Figure 3: Business Ethics and Sports Program Ethics

Traditional Businesses	Coaching/Program Administration
Human Resource Planning and Staffing	Student-Athlete Recruiting
Employee Development	Athlete Training
Human Resource Educational Issues	Student-Athlete Academic Requirements
Financial Management	Financial Management
Governmental, Corporate, and Industry Reporting and Documentation	NCAA, NJCAA, NFL, MLB, NAIA Reporting and Documentation
Customer Relations	Fan Support/Alumni
Employee Safety and Welfare	Student-Athlete Safety and Welfare

Administrative Tip

A program that endorses social/ethical response tactics has visible side benefits. The program atmosphere will be optimistic, honest, altruistic, and healthy.

There are four social/ethical choices that managers and coaches can adopt from these ethical situations.

1. Social/Ethical Opposition: An approach to social/ethical responsibility in which the company/program/ manager/coach does as little as possible and often makes decisions that most people would recognize as not being in the best interest of society, the organization, or the people who have an interest in the organization.
2. Social/Ethical Obligation: An approach to social/ethical responsibility that the company/program/manager/coach just meets the minimum legal requirements.
3. Social/Ethical Reaction: An approach to social/ethical responsibilities in which the company/program/manager/coach goes beyond the bare minimum requirements if specifically asked to.
4. Social/Ethical Response: An approach to social/ethical responsibility in which the company/program/ manager/coach actively seeks opportunities to contribute to the well being of society, the organization, and the people in the organization. (Griffin and Ebert, 1993)

From the above four choices, the most proactive method is the Social/Ethical Response. If one is to implement this anticipatory methodology for confronting ethical situations, the most apropos tool to utilize is an ethical program plan and code of ethics.

Development of an Ethics Program

To begin with, an organization developing an ethical program and code of ethics must explore and scrutinize its values first. Values and ethics, though comparable, are two independent items. The relationship between ethics and values is that "values are core beliefs about what is intrinsically desirable. . . . [V]alues give rise to ideals and actions that are called ethics. . . . [E]thics require a decision-maker to consider the facts and actions in light of important internal values" (Guy, 1990).

Figure 4: Code of Ethics Factors (Guy, 1990)

Caring   Honesty   Loyalty

Fairness   Accountability   Promise Keeping

Integrity   Respect for Others

Respect for Citizenship   Pursuit of Excellence

From these essential abstractions, Mary Guy in her 1990 text, *Ethical Decision Making in Everyday Work Situations,* expounds on 10 core values, shown in Figure 4, that go into formulating an organization's code of ethics.

The depth and magnitude of these subjective core values totally depends on what the program deems intrinsically desirable. Once one has examined the program's philosophical base, then one can develop and implement an ethical program plan.

Figure 5: Ethical Program Plan (Hall, 1993)

I. A Statement of Values
II. Corporate/Program Tradition and Values
III. Tone at the Top
IV. A Code of Conduct
V. Established Procedures
VI. Ethical Training Programs
VII. Hot Line/Open Door Policy
VIII. Ongoing Oversight Control

An ethical program plan is a written document that clarifies organizational values and gives miscellaneous rules that guide actions in as many foreseeable operational conditions as possible. There are eight ingredients that must be present in fostering and employing an ethical program plan:

Section I, Statement of Values, is the ethical equivalent to a business mission statement. This statement is a comprehensive narrative that is a broad basis for the program's ethical plan.

Administrative Tip

The core values of a program are the side effects of a coach's or program administrator's outlook toward ethical choices. Top-down flow is most evident in ethical core values. Consider oneself at the top. All ethical decisions from the top will be noted and continuously dissected as they flow down to the program's subordinates.

Sections II and III, Corporate/Program Tradition and Values and Tone at the Top, are historical overviews of past program ethical actions and values as well as of the current overall atmosphere in the profession and organization.

Sections IV, V, and VI, a Code of Conduct, Established Procedures, and Ethical Training Programs, are the determined, tangible codes and procedures for ethical action in the program. The more circumscribed and tangible one can be with each definitive procedure the better.

Sections VII and VIII, Hot Line/Open Door Policy and Oversight/Control, are the overseeing and monitoring directives in an ethical program plan.

Summary

A person's ethical behavior is shaped by numerous historical influences. Coaches and program administrators can regulate and manage individual ethical decisions by planning for and structuring program ethical expectations. A coach, along with his or her internal stakeholders (players and staff), should clarify the program values that, in turn, guide ethical program decisions and actions. While player and staff meetings that reiterate principles and expectations are significant in accentuating program philosophies, a written ethical program plan should be utilized to eliminate any possible misconceptions and individual ethical choice deviations.

SECTION V: Appendix

Entrepreneurship and Coaching

Successful entrepreneurs are individuals who are opportunistic and exploitive. While the connotation for the words *opportunistic* and *exploitive* is not always encouraging, here they are a positive trait. Entrepreneurs envision the future and take advantage of the potential conditions sometimes only they can anticipate and foresee. They derive personal satisfaction not only from making a profit but also from realizing their intrinsic goals. For some entrepreneurs, profit is a secondary consideration. Their inner drive to accomplish objectives gives them a self-confidence that permits them to take risks that others would consider and avoid.

There are actually three types of entrepreneurs:

1. Artisan Entrepreneur—A person who starts a business with primary technical skill and little business knowledge.
2. Opportunistic Entrepreneur—A person who starts a business with both sophisticated managerial skill and technical knowledge.
3. Entrepreneurial Team—This is two or more individuals who work together as entrepreneurs to complement each other. (Longenecker, Moore, and Petty, 2002)

These three classifications are crucial to understand as a prospective entrepreneur. Simply stated, a coach or program administrator needs to know what type and level of entrepreneur he or she is in order to distinguish his or her future potential and limitations. Not consciously accepting one's current limitations could be the ultimate factor in the demise of one's impending entrepreneurial operation.

There is a new resurgence in small business ownership, and the coaching profession is no different than any other. The two primary types of entrepreneurial ventures for coaches are consulting and instructional camps.

Consulting

Consulting, in its most original form, is selling one's proficiency and intelligence in a discipline to another individual or organization that needs it. From a more technical standpoint, consultants are "people who have an expertise in a specific area or areas and offer unbiased opinions and advise for a fee... a consultant is not an employee but an independent contractor" (Gray, 1986). The depth and intensity of one's consulting business depends greatly on ambition and expectations. As coaches, our consulting enterprise can be as casual as helping colleagues with general, informal advice and insight or as official as setting up a separate business entity, establishing a proposal sales system, initiating wide-ranging marketing activities, or structuring our consulting procedures, etc.

Before taking into consideration the challenges of being a consultant, a coach or program administrator must consider the "exceptional value" that he or she can offer as a coach. Ask questions:

- Do I truly have the level of knowledge and comprehension of my particular coaching specialty to provide a benefit to other coaches?
- Do I have good written and oral skills?
- Am I completion oriented?
- Can I be objective and unbiased in my consultation?
- Am I a good instructor?
- Am I willing to accept the hard work that goes along with being a consultant?
- Can I maintain a high level of confidentiality?
- Am I a skillful time manager?
- Can I market and sell myself and my services?
- Do I have the aptitude to observe, analyze, and then solve problems?
- Do I have the financial resources to initiate a consulting venture?
- Where will my clients come from? What is my market niche and targeted segment?
- Will my target market of clients be potentially profitable?
- How much worth can I place on my services?
- What is the competitive atmosphere for coaching consultants?

These are just a few of the daunting questions one will have to ask before jumping into consulting. The upside of launching and operating a consulting venture is substantial. In general, most of the start-up overhead is limited to basic office equipment and promotion of the venture. The work is very dynamic and differs from situation to situation. Finally, facilitating someone else's achievement has very ample intrinsic rewards.

If one feels that functioning as an entrepreneurial coaching consultant would be desirable, one should utilize the business concepts in this text to set up, plan, and manage the operation.

Instructional Camps

From our distinct coaching outlook, the most popular venue in which to express our "entrepreneurial spirit" is instructional camps and clinics. If one wants to thrive in these small business ventures, there are some recognized keys that are universal to all sports camps and clinics. The ensuing directives are in no particular arrangement and will need to be focused explicitly on one's particular sport and its precise operating methodology.

1. It is strongly recommended to regard all camp operations (and all entrepreneurial undertakings) as absolutely separate from one's core coaching job. To integrate camp operations with the program's normal processes could be at best confusing and at worst destructive.

2. Follow the indispensable managerial principals (discussed in Chapters 1-5) in conducting all camp business. All of the business theories and practices that pertain to one's athletic program also apply to one's camp venture.

3. It is soundly recommended that the camp business be incorporated. Incorporation creates a distinct, separate business entity with a life of its own. The primary advantage to incorporating is that the coach is or program administrator's personal liability, as a rule, is limited to the corporation and excludes his or her personal assets. The foremost disadvantage is double taxation. Not only is the camp business taxed but any income that one derives from the camp operation will then also be taxed. Confer with a tax accountant about the implications and set up of the camp corporation.

4. Never forget: *The customer is everything*. All of one's camp aspirations and actions should always derive from this.

5. For fruition and future camp expansion, offer superior customer satisfaction to all camp attendees. To do this, provide the highest quality product one's resources can provide. This, in turn, will generate positive word of mouth and enhance future operations.

6. Under the same foundations as quality, hire the most competent staff and instructors. Their compensation should fit and (if the resources allow) surpass their expectations. Supply camp staff with additional perks to retain them for future camp seasons.

7. Be hands-on and visible at camp sessions. Even if one is not acting as a clinician, walk the facility and communicate with the participants. Show an allegiance and commitment to the product.

8. Have a structured, controlled camp atmosphere. It will convey professionalism as well as lessen campers' anxieties. Post schedules and instructional sites whenever possible. Additionally, have precamp staff conferences to scrutinize schedules, locations, activities, and job responsibilities. The more systematic the camp business, the better "flow" and atmosphere the camp will have.

9. At the end of each camp, survey the campers (either informally though walk-around discussions or formally through survey techniques). Ask them about their experiences at camp and what other services and training they may perhaps want in the future. If the parents are involved, solicit their assessments. Additionally, enlist the camp staff in a "recap session" and get their input. Feedback is the salient key to improving quality in the future.

10. Keep the camper-to-staff ratio as low as is financially practical. The lower the ratio, the more superior the customized quality of the camp.

11. Develop an appealing, enlightening camp brochure. Triple-check all final prints before circulating it to the public. Once again, the up-front financial resources and camp projections will shape a great part of the promotional and admission brochures.

12. Follow a stringent risk management philosophy (imparted in Chapter 12). Be, if anything, overinsured.

13. Maintain the most advantageous, straightforward recordkeeping system. Utilize any number of computer software programs for precise accounting. Plan on the camp being audited. This attitude will

intensify the camp's system integrity. If one is not detail oriented, outsource this administration function to someone who is. Medical records; insurance forms; emergency contact information; employment contracts; and specialized, sports-specific information are all detail-oriented materials that need compulsory maintenance. Special note: By no means consent to a child or clinic member participating in any event or activity without his or her entire records being on file. This could be construed as gross negligence and may be a cause for loss of protection under the camps insurance carrier.

14. Have top skilled training and medical personnel on staff. Have them assist in all medical and insurance considerations.

Other alternatives one would need to contemplate are more sports-specific and personal. Items such as

- Operating of day camps or overnight camps.
- Providing food plans or having campers independently obtain food.
- Running specialty camps or administering comprehensive, overall skill camps.
- Running an all-inclusive, total camper session or breaking down the camp into age and skill groups.
- Allowing camp sessions to be open to the general public or closing training sessions.
- Providing auxiliary activities or keeping the camps sports-specific only.

All of these issues (and more) are the individualized concerns of one's camp and necessitate planned strategies.

SECTION V: Appendix Bibliography

Bellman, Geoffrey M. 1990. *The consultants calling*. San Francisco: Jossey Bass.

Bond, William J. 1997. *Going solo: Developing a home based consulting business from the ground up*. New York: McGraw-Hill.

Bermont, Hubert. 1989. *How to become a successful consultant in your own field*. Rocklin, CA: Prima.

Gray, Douglas A. 1986. *Start and run a profitable consulting business*. British Columbia, Canada: International Self-Counsel Press.

Hill, Charles W. L., and Gareth R. Jones. 2001. *Strategic management: An integrated approach*. Boston: Houghton-Mifflin.

Holtz, Herman. 1999. *The concise guide to becoming an independent consultant*. New York: John Wiley and Sons.

Karlson, David. 1988. *Marketing your consulting or professional services*. Menlo Park, CA: Crisp Publications.

Longenecker, Justin G., Carlos W. Moore, and J. William Petty. 2002. *Small business management: An entrepreneurial emphasis*. Cincinnati: South-Western Publishing.

Shenson, Howard L., and Jerry R. Wilson. 1993. *138 quick ideas to get more clients*. New York: John Wiley and Sons.

Tuller, Lawrence W. 1992. *The independent consultants Q&A book*. Holbrook, MA: Bob Adams.

SECTION VI: Suggested Readings

Advertising

Granat, Jay P. 1994. *Persuasive advertising for entrepreneurs and small business owners.* New York: Hawthorne Press.

Hahn, Fred E., and Kenneth G. Mangun. 1997. *Do it yourself advertising and promotion.* New York: John Wiley and Sons.

Jackall, Robert, and Janice M. Hirota. 2000. *Image makers.* Chicago: University of Chicago Press.

Budgeting

Dickey, Terry. 1994. *Budgeting for small businesses.* Menlo Park, CA: Crisp.

Finney, Robert G. 1993. *Powerful budgeting for better planning and management.* New York: AMA-COM.

Shim, Jae K., Joel G. Siegel, and Abraham J. Simon. 1996. *Handbook of budgeting for non-profit organizations.* Englewood Cliffs, NJ: Prentice Hall.

Tracy, John A. 1996. *The fast forward M.B.A. in finance.* New York: John Wiley and Sons.

Consulting

Bond, William J. 1997. *Going solo: Develop a home-based consulting business from the ground up.* New York: McGraw-Hill.

Gray, Douglas A. 1996. *Start and run a profitable consulting business.* North Vancouver, Canada: Self-Counsel.

Holtz,. Herman. 1999. *The concise guide to becoming an independent consultant.* New York: John Wiley and Sons.

Shenson, Howard L., aznd Jerry R. Wilson. 1993. *138 quick ideas to get more clients.* New York: John Wiley and Sons.

Control

Brokaw, Leslie. 1995. *301 great management ideas.* Boston: INC Publishing.

Evans, James R. 1999. *The management and control of quality.* Cincinnati: South-Western Publishing.

Ethics

Boatright, John R. 1997. *Ethics and the conduct of business.* Upper Saddle River, NJ: Prentice Hall.

Pratley, Peter. 1995. *The essence of business ethics.* London: Prentice Hall.

Preiffer, Raymond S., and Ralph P. Forsberg. 2000. *Ethics on the job.* Belmont, CA: Wadsworth.

Velasquez, Manual G. 2002. *Business ethics: Concepts and cases.* Upper Saddle River, NJ: Prentice Hall.

Fundraising

Allen, Judy. 2000. *Event planning: The ultimate guide to successful meetings, corporate events, fundraising galas.* New York: John Wiley and Sons.

Edles, L. Peter. 1992. *Fundraising.* New York: McGraw-Hill.

Flanagan, Joan. 1999. *Successful fundraising: A complete handbook for volunteers and professionals.* New York: McGraw-Hill.

General Management

Boyett, Joseph, and Jimmy Boyett. 1998. *The guru guide: The best ideas of the top management thinkers.* New York: John Wiley and Sons.

Crainer, Stuart. 1999. *The 75 greatest management decisions ever made…and the 21 worst.* New York: AMACOM.

Drucker, Peter F. 1999. *Management challenges for the 21st century.* New York: Harpers.

Human Resource Management

DeVine George. 1997. *Managing your employees.* Englewood Cliffs, NJ: Prentice Hall.

Murphy, Kevin R., Jeanette N. Cleveland. *Understanding performance appraisals.* Thousand Oaks, CA: Sage.

O'Connor, Bridget N. Michael Bronner, and Chester Delaney. 1996. *Training for organizations.* Cincinnati: South-Western Publishing.

Wilson, Robert F. 1997. *Conducting better job interviews.* New York: Barrons.

Leadership

Blanchard, Ken, John P. Carlos, and Alan Randolph. 1996. *Empowerment takes more than a minute.* San Francisco: Berrett-Koehler.

Peters, Tom. 1994. *The pursuit of wow!* New York: Vintage Books.

Putzier, John. 2001. *Get weird!: 101 innovative ways to make your company a great place to work.* New York: AMACOM.

Quigley, Joseph V. 1993. *Vision: How leaders develop it, share it, and sustain it.* New York: McGraw-Hill.

Marketing

Cook, Kenneth J. 1993. *Small business marketing.* Lincolnwood, IL: NTC Business Books.

Hingston, Peter. 2001. *Effective marketing.* New York: Dorling Kindersley.

Luther, William M. 2001. *The marketing plan.* New York: AMACOM.

Muckian, Michael. 2001. *Prentice Hall's one-day M.B.A. in marketing.* Paramus, NJ: Prentice Hall.

Organization

Bruce, Raymond, and Sherman Wyman. 1998. *Changing organizations: Practice, action, training and research.* Thousand Oaks, CA: Sage.

Cell, Edward. 1998. *Organizational life: Learning to be self directed.* Lanham, MD: University Press of America.

Hellrieger, Don, John Slocum, and Richard W. Woodman. 2001. *Organizational behavior.* Cincinnati: South-Western Publishing.

Planning

Barrow, Paul. 2001. *The best laid business plans: How to write them, how to pitch them.* London: Virgin.

Henricks, Mark. 1999. *Business plans made easy.* Irvine, CA: Entrepreneur Media.

Pinson, Linda. 2001. *The anatomy of a business plan.* Chicago: Dearborn.

Public Relations

Chajet, Clive, and Tom Shachtman. 1991. *Image by design.* Reading, MA: Addison-Wesley.

Haig, Matt. 2000. *The essential guide to public relations on the internet.* London: Kogan Page.

Marconi, Joe. 1996. *Image marketing: Using public perceptions to attain business objectives.* Lincolnwood, IL: NTC.

Risk Management

Goodden, Randall L. 1996. *Preventing and handling product liability.* New York: Marcel Dekker.

Hopkins, Bruce R. 1994. *Nonprofit law dictionary.* New York: John Wiley and Sons.

Nader, Ralph, and Wesley J. Smith. 1990. *Winning the insurance game.* New York: Knightsbridge.

Stettner, Morey. 1994. *Buyers beware: How to win at the insurance game.* (Chicago: Probus.

Strategic Management

Heller, Robert. 2000. *Peter Drucker: The great pioneer of management theory and practice.* New York: Dorling-Kindersley.

Heller, Robert. 2000. *Tom Peters: The best selling prophet of the management revolution.* New York: Dorling-Kindersley.

Hickman, Craig R. 1994. *The strategy game.* New York: McGraw-Hill.

Hindle, Tim. 1994. *Field guide to strategy.* Boston: Harvard Business.

Jocobs, Robert W. 1994. *Real time strategic change.* San Francisco: Berrett-Koehler.

References ········

Abrahams, J. (1995). *The mission statement book*. Berkeley, CA: Ten Speed Press.

Adams, J. D. (1986). *Transformational leadership: From vision to results*. Alexandria, VA: Miles River Press.

Agor, W. H. (1989). *Intuition in organizations*. Newberry Park, CA: Sage.

Alesandrini, K. (1992). *Survive information overload*. Homewood, IL: Business One.

American Marketing Association: Committee on Definitions. (1960). *Marketing definitions: A glossary of marketing terms*. Chicago: American Medical Association.

Baird, J. E. (1977). *The dynamics of organizational communication*. New York: Harper and Row.

Baird, J. E., & Stull, J. B. (1988). *Business communication: Strategies and solutions*. New York: McGraw Hill.

Batten, J. D. (1989). *Tough-minded leadership*. New York: American Marketing Association, AMA-COM.

Becker, F., & Steele, F. (1995). *Workplace by design*. San Francisco: Jossey Bass.

Bedeian, A. G. (1993). *Management*. Fort Worth, TX: Dryden Press.

Belch, G. E., & Belch, M. A. (1998). *Advertising and promotion: An integrated marketing communication perspective*. Boston: Irwin-McGraw Hill.

Bennett, P. D. (1988). *Dictionary of marketing terms*. Chicago: American Marketing Association, AMACOM.

Berkowitz, E. N., Kerin, R. A., Hartley, S. W., & Rudelius, W. (1992). *Marketing*. Homewood, IL: Irwin.

Blake, R. R., & Mouton, J. S. (1978). *The managerial grid*. Houston, TX: Gulf Publishing.

Bohlander, G., Snell, S., & Sherman, A. (2001). *Managing human resources*. Cincinnati, OH: South-Western Publishing.

Booher, D. (1985). *Cutting paperwork in the corporate culture*. New York: Facts on File.

Boone, L. E., & Kurtz, D. L. (1995). *Contemporary marketing plus*. Fort Worth, TX: Dryden Press.

Broce, T. E. (1986). *Fundraising: The guide to raising money from private sources*. Normand, OK: University of Oklahoma Press.

Butler, J. E., Ferris, G. R., & Napeir, N. K. (1991). *Strategy and human resource management*. Cincinnati, OH: South-Western Publishing.

Carlisle, H. M. (1987). *Management essentials*. Chicago: Science and Research Associates.

Certo, S. C. (1994). *Modern management*. Boston: Allyn and Bacon.

Certo, S. C., & Peter, J. P. (1990). *Strategic management: A focus on process*. New York: McGraw-Hill.

Cheek, L. M. (1977). *Zero-base budgeting comes of age*. New York: American Marketing Association, AMACOM.

Chisholm, D. (1989). *Coordination without hierarchy: Informal structures in multi-organizational systems*. Berkeley, CA: University of California Press.

Churchill, G. A., & Peter, J. P. (1998). *Marketing: Creating value for customers*. Boston: Irwin-McGraw Hill.

Cohen, W. A. (1990). *The art of the leader*. Englewood Cliffs, NJ: Prentice Hall.

Collier, A. T. (1992), March/April). Business leadership in a creative society. *Harvard Business Review,* 159.

Conger, J. A. (1989). *The charismatic leader*. San Francisco: Jossey Bass.

Cooper, R. K. (1991). *The performance edge*. Boston: Houghton Mifflin.

Crain, D. P. (1986). *Personnel: The management of human resources*. Boston: Kent.

Cummings, T. C. (1980). *Systems theory for organizational development*. New York: John Wiley and Sons.

David, F. R. (1997). *Strategic management*. Upper Saddle, NJ: Prentice Hall.

DeNisi, A. S., & Griffin, R. W. (2001). *Human resource management*. Boston: Houghton Mifflin.

Dessler, G. (1997). *Human resource management*. Upper Saddle River, NJ: Prentice Hall.

DiGaetani, J. L. (1986). *The handbook of executive communication*. Homewood, IL: Dow-Jones-Irvin.

Dilenschneider, R. L., & Forrestal, D. J. (1987). *The Dartnell public relations handbook*. Chicago: Dartnell.

Donnelly, J. H., Gibon, J. L., & Ivancevich, J. M. (1987). *Fundamentals of management*. Plano, TX: Business Publication.

Dressier, G. (1982). *Organization and management*. Reston, VA: Reston Publishing.

DuBrin, A. J. (2003). *Essentials of management*. Mason, OH: Thompson &-Western.

Evans, J. R., & Berryman, B. (1997). *Marketing*. Englewood Cliffs, NJ: Prentice Hall.

Evans, J. R., & Berryman, B. (1984). *Essentials of marketing*. New York: McMillian.

Finney, R. G. (1994). *Basics of budgeting*. New York: American Medical Association.

Finney, R. G. (1993). *Powerful budgeting for better planning and management*. New York: American Medical Association.

Fisher, C. D., Schoenfeldt, L. F., & Shaw, J. B. (1999) *Human resource management*. Boston: Houghton Mifflin.

Flanagan, J. (1982). *The grass roots fund raising book*. Chicago: Contemporary Books.

French, W. L. (1994). *Human resource management*. Boston: Houghton-Mifflin.

Friedman, J. P. (1987). *Barron's dictionary of business terms*. Hauppage, NY: Barron's Educational Series.

Friedman, J. P. (1987). *Dictionary of business terms*. Hauppauge, NY: Barrons.

Galbraith, J. R. (1978). *Organizational design*. Reading MA: Addison-Wesley.

Garcia, J. E., & Haggith, C. (1990, September). Organizational development: Interventions that work. *Personnel Administrator,* 90-92.

Grasty, W. K., & Sheinkept, K. G. (1982). *Successful fundraising*. New York: Charles Scribner and Sons.

Gray, J. L., & Starke, F. A. *Organizational behavior: concepts and applications*. Columbus, OH: Merril, 1988.

Griffin, R. W., & Moorehead, G. (1986). *Organizational behavior*. Boston: Houghton Mifflin.

Griffin, R. W. (1996). *Management*. Boston; Houghton Mifflin.

Griffin, R. W. (1990). *Management*. Boston: Houghton Mifflin.

Griffin, R. W., & Ebert, R. J. (1993). *Business*. Englewood Cliffs, NJ: Prentice Hall.

Gumpert, D. (1990). *How to really create a successful business plan*. Boston: NC Publishing.

Guy, M. E. (1990). *Ethical decision making in everyday work situations*. n: Quorum Books.

Hackman, M. A., & Johnson, C. E. (1991). *Leadership: A communication perspective*. Prospect Heights, IL: Waveland.

Hahn, F. E. (1993). *Do it yourself advertising and promotion*. New York: John Wiley and Sons.

Hall, W. D. (1993). *Making the right decision: Ethics for managers*. New York: John Wiley and Sons.

Hamilton, C., & Parker, C. (1987). *Communication for results*. Belmont, CA: Wadsworth.

Harrel, G. D., & Frazier, G. L. (1999). *Marketing: Connecting with customers*. Upper Saddle River, NJ: Prentice Hall.

Harris, D. A., Engen, B. W., & Fitch, W. E. *Planning and designing the office environment*. New York: Van Nostrand, 1991.

Hart, N. A. (1988). *Practical advertising and publicity*. London: McGraw Hill.

Hellriegel, D., Slocum, J. W., & Woodman, R. W. (1986). *Organizational behavior*. St. Paul, MN: West.

Hersey, P., & Blanchard, K. H. (1982). *Management of organizational behavior*. Englewood Cliffs, NJ: Prentice Hall.

Hiam, A. (1997). *Marketing for dummies*. Foster City, CA: For Dummies.

Hill, C. W. L., & Jones, G. R. (2000). *Strategic management: An integrated approach*. Boston: Houghton Mifflin.

Hill, C. W., & Jones, G. R. (2001). *Strategic management: An integrated approach*. Boston: Houghton Mifflin.

Hindle, T. (1994). *Field guide to strategy*. Boston: Harvard Business School Press.

Hingston, P. (2001). *Effective marketing*. New York: Dorling Kindersley.

Hisrich, R. D. (1990). *Marketing*. New York: Barron's Business.

Hodgetts, R. M. (1999). *Modern human relations at work*. Fort Worth, TX: Dryden Press.

Holt, D. H. (1990). *Management: Principles and Practices*. Englewood Cliffs, NJ: Prentice Hall.

House, R. J., & Mitchell T.R. (1974, May). Path glory theory of leadership. *Journal of Contemporary Business*.

Janus, L. R., & Jones, S. K. (1982). *Time management for executives*. New York: Charles Scribner and Sons.

Jefkins, F. (1993). *Planned press and public relations*. London: Blackie Academic and Professional.

Jennings, M. M., & Shipper, F. (1989). *Avoiding and surviving law suits*. San Francisco: Jossey Bass.

Jucius, M., Dietzer, B., & Schlender, W. (1973). *Elements of managerial action*. Homewood, IL: Irwin.

Kast, F. E., & Rosenzweig, J. E. (1979). *Organization and management: A system and contingency approach*. New York: McGraw-Hill.

Kaueyer, Richard A. (1982). *Planning and using a total personnel system*. New York: Van Nostrand-Reinhold.

Keding, A., & Bivins, T. (1990). *How to produce creative advertising*. Lincolnwood, IL: National Textbook Company.

Kendall, R. (1996). *Public relations campaign strategies*. New York: Harper Collins.

Kinnear, T. C., Bernhardt, K. L., Krentler, K. A. (1995). *Principles of marketing*. New York: Harper Collins.

Kotler, Philip. (1994). *Marketing management*. Englewood Cliffs, NJ: Prentice Hall.

Kotler, Philip. (1994). *Marketing management: Analysis, planning, implementation, and control*. Englewood Cliffs, NJ: Prentice Hall.

Kotler, P., & Armstrong, G. (1993). *Marketing: An introduction*. Englewood Cliffs, NJ: Prentice Hall.

Kotler, P., & Armstrong, Gary. (1997). *Marketing: An introduction*. Upper Saddle River, NJ: Prentice Hall.

Kotter, J. P. (1988). *The leadership factor*. New York: Free Press.

Kouze, J. M., & Posner, B. Z. (1999). *The leadership challenge*. San Francisco: Jossey Bass.

Kouze, J. M., & Posner, B. Z. (1997). *The leadership challenge*. San Francisco: Jossey Bass.

Kreitner, R. (1995). *Management*. Boston: Houghton Mifflin.

Lamb, C. W., Hair, J. F., & McDaniel, C. (1992). *Principles of marketing*. Cincinnati, OH: South-Western Publishing.

Lane, Marc J. (1989). *Legal handbook for small businesses*. New York: American Marketing Association, AMACOM.

Lasner, W. (1994). *The perfect business plan made simple*. New York: Doubleday.

Laurie, J. (1990, March). The ABC's of change management. *Training and Development Journal*, 87-88.

Longnecker, J. G., Moore, C. W., & Petty, J. W. (2002). *Small business management: An entrepreneurial emphasis*. Cincinnati, OH: South-Western Publishing.

Luck, D. J., & Ferrel, O. C. (1985). *Marketing strategies and plans*. Englewood Cliffs, NJ: Prentice Hall.

Lyden, D. P., Reitzel, J. D., & Roberts, N. J. *Business and the law*. New York: McGraw-Hill, 1985.

McDonald, M. H. B., & Keegan, W. J. (1997). *Marketing plans that work*. Newton, MA: Butterworth-Heinemann.

Mallory, C. (1989). *Publicity power: A practical guide to effective promotions*. Menlo Park, CA: Crisp Publications.

Manz, C. C., & Simms, H. P. (1989). *Super leadership*. New York: Berkeley Books.

Maslow, A. (1954). *Motivation and personality*. New York: Harper Row.

Mayer, J. J. (1995). *Time management for dummies*. Foster City, CA: For Dummies.

McCarthy, E. J., & Perreault, W. D. (1994). *Essentials of marketing: A global managerial approach*. Burr Ridge, IL: Irwin.

McGhee, W. (1977). Training and development theory: Policies and practices. In *A.S.P.A. handbook of personnel and industry relations, Volume 5*. Washington, DC: Bureau of National Affairs.

McGregor, D. (1960). *The human side of the enterprise*. New York: McGraw Hill.

Megginson, L. C., Mosley, D. C., & Pietri, P. H. (1983). *Management: Concepts and applications.* Cambridge, MA: Harper and Row.

Mescon, M. H., Albert, M., & Khedouri, F. (1983). *Management: Individual and organizational effectiveness.* Cambridge, MA: Harper and Row.

Milkovich, G. T., & Boudreau, J. W. (1991). *Human resource management.* Homewood, IL: Irwin.

Miller, L. K. *Sports business management.* Gaithersburg, MD: Aspen Publishing, 1997.

Miller, R. L., & Jentz, G. A. (1999) *Fundamentals of business law.* Austin, TX: West Publishing.

Mintzberg, H. (1983). *Power in and around organizations.* Englewood Cliffs, NJ: Prentice Hall.

Mintzberg, H. (1994).*The rise and fall of strategic planning.* New York; Free Press.

Monday R. W., Holmes, R. E. & Flippo, E. B. (1983). *Management concepts and practices.* Boston: Allyn and Bacon.

Murphy, H. A., & Hildebrant, H. W. (1988). *Effective business communication.* New York: McGraw Hill.

Murphy, P. E. (1998). *80 exemplary ethical statements.* Notre Dame, IN: University of Notre Dame Press.

Nanus, B. (1989). *The leader's edge.* Chicago: Contemporary Books.

Nystrom, P. C., & Starbuck, W. H. (1981). *Handbook of organizational design volume 2: Remodeling organizations and their environments.* London, England, Oxford Press.

O'Brien, J. A. (1994). *Introduction to information systems.* Burr Ridge, IL: Irwin.

Page, S. B. (1984). *Business policies and procedures handbook.* Englewood Cliffs, NJ: Prentice Hall.

Parkhouse, B. L. (1996). *The management of sport.* St. Louis, MO: Mosby.

Pearce, J. A., & Robinson, R. B. (1989). *Management.* New York: Random House.

Peterson, R. B., & Lane T. (1979). *Systematic management of human resources.* Reading, MA: Addison-Wesley.

Pollar, O. (1992). *Organizing your workspace.* Menlo, CA: Crisp Publications.

Porter, M. E. (1985). *Competitive advantage: Creating and sustaining superior performance.* New York: Free Press.

Porter, M. E. (1980). *Competitive strategy.* New York: Free Press.

Pride, W. M., & Ferrell, O. C. (1993). *Marketing concepts and strategies.* Boston: Houghton Mifflin.

Pride, W. P., Hughes, R. J., & Kapoor, J. R. (2000). *Business.* Boston: Houghton Mifflin.

Rachlin, R., & Sweeny, H. W. A. (1994). *Handbook of budgeting.* New York: John Wiley and Sons.

Ramacitti, D. F. (1990). *Do-it-yourself publicity.* New York: American Marketing Association, AMA-COM.

Ramsey, J. E., & Ramsey, I. L. (1985). *Budgeting basics.* New York: Franklin Watts.

Rich, S. R., & Gumpert, D. (1987). *Business plans that win $$.* New York: Harpers Row.

Robertson, I. (1987). *Sociology.* New York: W. H. Freeman & Company.

Rothwell, W. J., & Kazanas, H. C. (1988). *Strategic human resource planning and management.* Englewood Cliffs, NJ: Prentice Hall.

Rue, L. W., & Byars, L. L. (1992). *Management: Skills and applications.* Homewood, IL: Irwin.

Schermerhorn, J. R., & Hunt, J. G. (1988). *Managing organizational behavior.* New York: John Wiley and Sons.

Schewe, C. D., & Hiam, A. W. (1998). *The portable M.B.A. in marketing.* New York: John Wiley and Sons.

Schmidt, W. H., & Finnigan, J. P. (1993). *T Q Manager: A practical guide for managing in a total quality organization.* San Francisco: Jossey Bass.

Schoell, W. F., & Guiltman, J. P. (1988). *Marketing: Contemporary concepts and practices.* Boston: Allyn and Bacon.

Schoell, W. F., & Guiltman, J. P. (1995). *Marketing: Contemporary concepts and practices.* Boston: Allyn and Bacon.

Smith, J. (1991). *The publicity kit: A complete guide for entrepreneurs, small businesses and non-profit organizations.* New York: John Wiley and Sons.

Smith, L. Y., & Roberson, G. G. (1985). *Business law, 6th edition.* St. Paul, MN: West Publishing.

Soderberg, N. R. (1986). *Public relations for the entrepreneur and growing business.* Chicago: Probus.

Stanton, W. J., Etzel, M. J., & Walker, B. J. (1994). *Fundamentals of marketing.* New York: McGraw Hill.

Stearns, T. M., & Aldag, R. J. (1987). *Management.* Cincinnati, OH: South-Western Publishing.

Stedry, A. C. (1990). *Budget control and cost behavior.* Englewood Cliffs, NJ: Prentice Hall.

Steinmetz, L. L., & Todd, R. H. (1986). *First line management: Approaching supervision effectively.* Homewood, IL: Irwin.

Stoner, J. A. F. (1978). *Management*. Englewood Cliffs, NJ: Prentice Hall.

Sudhalter, D. L. (1980). *The management option*. New York: Human Services Press.

Synder, N. H., Dowd, J. J., & Houghton, D. M. (1994). *Vision, values, and courage: Leadership for quality management*. New York: Free Press.

Szilagy, A. (1981). *Management and performance*. Santa Monica, CA: Goodyear.

Tannenbaum, R., Margulies, N., & Massarik, F. (1985). *Human systems development*. San Francisco: Jossey-Bass.

Tiffany, P., & Peterson, S. D. (1997). *Business plans for dummies*. Foster City, CA: For Dummies.

Tracy, J. A. (1997). *Accounting for dummies*. Foster City, IL: For Dummies.

Trewatha, R. L., & Newport, M. G. (1979). *Management: Function and behavior*. Dallas TX: Business Publication.

Wallace, C. W. (1990). *Great ad! Low-cost, do-it-yourself advertising for your small business*. Blue Ridge Summit, PA: Liberty Hall Press.

Weinstein, A. (1994). *Market segmentation*. Chicago: Probus.

Wells, W., Burnett, J., & Moriarty, S. (1992). *Advertising principles and practices*. Englewood Cliffs, NJ: Prentice Hall.

Werther, W. B., & Davis, K. (1989). *Human resource and personnel management*. New York: McGraw-Hill.

Westwood, J. *The marketing plan: A practitioners guide*. Dover, NH: Kogan Page, 1998.

Wilcox, D. L., Ault, P. H., & Agee, W. K. (1998). *Public relations: Strategies and tactics*. New York: Longman Publishing.

Williams, C. (2000). *Management*. Cincinnati, OH: South-Western Publishing.

Winston, S. (1985). *The organized executive*. New York: Warner Books.

Wright, P., Pringle, C. D., & Kroll, M. J. (1994). *Strategic management: Text and cases*. Boston: Allyn and Bacon.

Young, A. (1986). *The management handbook*. New York: Crown Publishing.

About
the Author ....

A native of Pittsburgh, PA, Leonard earned his bachelors degree in accounting from Robert Morris College. He received an MBA in management from Tampa College and his doctorate in administration and management from Walden University. He has served as a regional tournament director and an independent summer camp entrepreneur, and has authored numerous national articles on sports administration. He is US Volleyball CAP Level II certified and US Volleyball Critical Thinking Seminar certified. He has also achieved his ACEP certification.

Over the past three years, in addition to his coaching duties, Dr. Leonard has served as a professor of business for the American InterContinental University in Atlanta. He has taught classes in entrepreneurship, all levels of management, and a range of marketing classes. His adjunct teaching experience in business dates back to 1989.

At the time of this printing, Dr. Richard Leonard will be entering his 7th season as the Head Women's Volleyball Coach at Georgia State University. Under Leonard, the Lady Panthers have been the most successful volleyball program in the school's history; Dr. Leonard, whose career record as a head coach stands at 144-69, holds the best winning percentage in school history at .676. For his efforts, Dr. Leonard was named Conference Coach of the Year in 2000, 2001, and 2003.

Prior to Georgia State, Leonard spent four seasons as the Associate Head Coach at St. Louis University. During his tenure at Saint Louis University, the Billikens developed into one of the best volleyball program in the midwest. They compiled a 91-59 mark including a 29-10 record and a trip to the Volleyball NIT.

Leonard was a member and player in the United States Volleyball Association from 1980 to 1997 and was AA rated. He has been on four USVB regional championship teams and seven USVB semifinalist and finalists. During his playing career, his teams have won over 125 tournaments and league championships.